{Code Names} Betsy and Babe

A Memoir

The story of a young couple teaching in
Kenya recruited to spy for the CIA
in the seventies.

Linda Shields Allison

BookLocker

Trenton, Georgia

Paperback ISBN: 978-1-959620-68-6
Hardcover ISBN: 978-1-959620-69-3
Ebook ISBN: 979-8-88531-815-0

Published by BookLocker.com, Inc., Trenton, Georgia.

BookLocker.com, Inc.
2024

First Edition

Library of Congress Cataloging in Publication Data
Allison, Linda Shields
{Code Names} Betsy and Babe: The story of a young couple teaching in Kenya recruited to spy for the CIA in the seventies by Linda Shields Allison
Library of Congress Control Number: 2024917001

{Code Names} **Betsy and Babe**

A Memoir

The story of a young couple teaching in Kenya recruited to spy for the CIA in the seventies.

Linda Shields Allison

This Memoir is Dedicated to

Shauna

Tara

and Joshua

Who Were With Us On Our

Incredible Journey in Kenya

And My Mom, Esther, Who
Saved Every Letter I Wrote to
Her During Our Extraordinary
Time in Kenya

Other Books by
Linda Shields Allison

The Emerald Bottle

The Bronze Bottle

The Amythyst Bottle

The Mandarin Bottle

The Turquoise Bottle

My Very Special
Thanks and Appreciation to
Terry Nettles Meaney and
Russell Mars for Your
Assisstance, Guidance, and
Support Throughout the
Process.
Your Advice and Validation
Encouraged Me to Share
The Story of Betsy and
Babe.

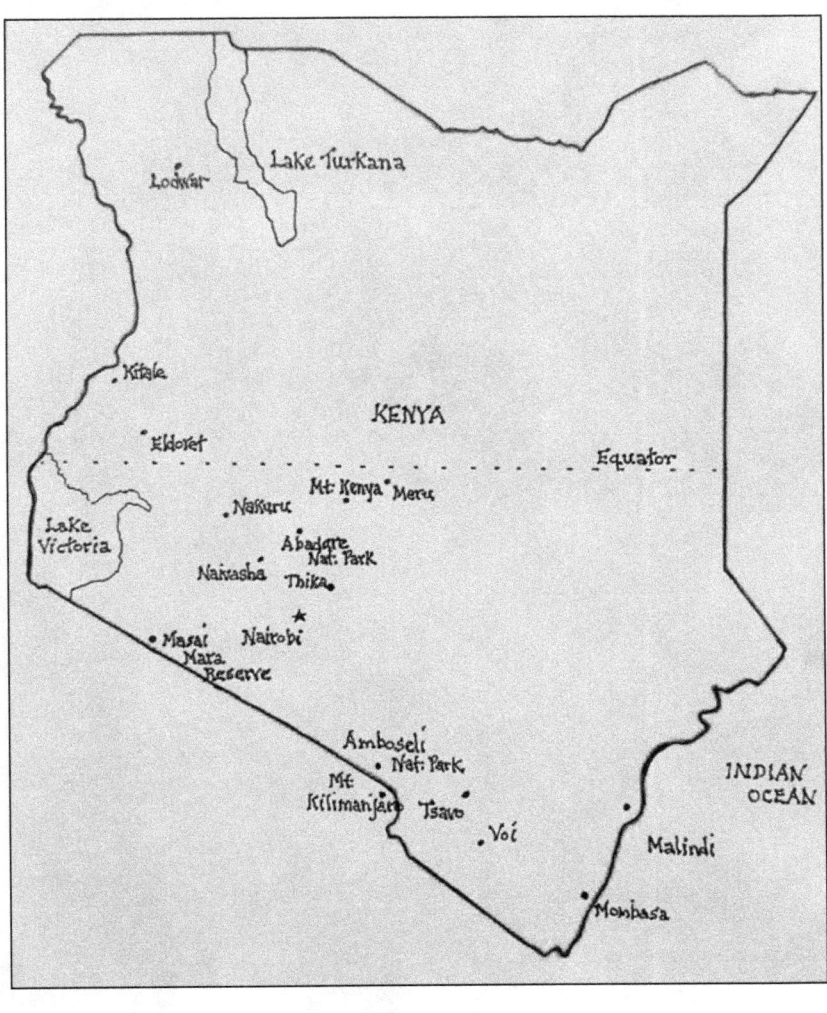

Lodwar

Lake Turkana

Kitale

KENYA

Eldoret

Equator

Mt. Kenya • Meru

Nakuru

Lake
Victoria

Aberdare
Nat. Park

Naivasha

Thika

★
Masai   Nairobi
Mara
Reserve

Amboseli
• Nat. Park

Mt.
Kilimanjaro   Tsavo

Voi

INDIAN
OCEAN

Malindi

Mombasa

The Coming of the Rains

A breeze whispers through the silent palms

chattering the cool green fronds together.

The mild breeze grows stronger, and the

palm fronds dip back and forth,

back and forth,

back and forth.

The first drop of rain splashes on the land

and is immediately absorbed into the sand.

They sink into the parched ground

and soon begin to fill the long dry rivers.

The land is wet, and the people are glad,

for the rains have begun.

Laura Schlesinger ~ 1972 — age 16

NIS Student ~ Class of 1973

Nairobi International School 1972

Prologue:
August 1971 ~ July 1976 – Nairobi, Kenya

I was twenty-five when we arrived in Kenya, and thirty-years-old when our family of five returned to California. I like to recall my time in Kenya as my *glory years*. I never looked better or felt more inspired. Living in the cosmopolitan city of Nairobi was incredible. I was a wife to my teacher husband, John, and the mother of two young girls, Shauna and Tara; our son Joshua would come three years later. Being in Kenya gave us the luxury to employ a houseboy, a gardener, and an ayah to help with the children—all for the ridiculous sum of one hundred dollars a month. This extra help afforded me the freedom to live an extraordinary and creative life—to meet remarkably adventurous people, who like us, had the courage to leave their comfortable lives and fly to Africa—a place some have labeled—*our darkest continent*. John was hired to teach at the American-run Nairobi International School. I worked part-time as a substitute teacher while raising our three children. What made our adventure even more astonishing was being recruited by the CIA to work undercover as spies for the American government under the code names: Betsy and Babe.

This all happened over fifty years ago. I'm in the twilight of my life now and wanted to write a few things down for my children, and perhaps others who were there with us, and maybe others who might just enjoy the adventure. The years of my life outside of Kenya seem all a bit muddled together into the sameness of everyday life. After Kenya, I loved my years working as an elementary school teacher in Hemet, California, and I have fond memories of my students and the many friends my husband and I shared our lives with. But as I sit at my desk recollecting the past, the five years of my life in Africa are vividly imprinted in my mind.

I remember picnics on Ngong Hills and flying kites with the children over the Great Rift Valley. I see majestic elephants and giraffes silhouetted against the beautiful equatorial sunsets on the grasslands of Nairobi Game Park—I hear the roar of a lion in the distance while camping in Tsavo National Game Park—I recall the raspy growl of hippos rising out of the water at dusk at Mzima Springs—I marvel at the sight of vast herds of zebra and gazelle grazing on the Serengeti savanna—I smell the briny salt air carried across the eastern winds of the Indian Ocean on safari to Mombasa—I envision the joy of African women, with young mtotos strapped on their backs, singing as they pick coffee along the road leading into Nairobi International School—I imagine the joy of young African boys pushing little homemade cars made from scraps of wire—I recollect the dignity of lean Masai men resting on their spears while herding cattle near their bomas—I marvel at the sight of huge jacaranda trees blanketing the city with lavender confetti each October—I sigh at the whispering song of wind rustling through thorn trees before a storm—My heart pulses at the sound of ancient tribal drums beating in my soul.

I envision a land—hauntingly magnificent—a land that guards its secrets well.

Chapter 1:
July, 1971 — A Fight and a Flight

'What are you talking about, John? Move to Kenya? Frankly, I'm so mad at you at the moment, I wouldn't *move* across the street with you!'

John gently grabbed my arm to prevent me from walking away from him. 'Please, Linda. Let me explain.'

We were standing outside my parents' house in San Diego, where we had been living with our two young daughters for two years. In 1969, my parents had graciously offered us their house while they moved to Japan to fulfill a two-year federal government contract my father had procured as a fire captain at Atsugi Naval Airbase. Their kind gesture was the break we needed. All we had to do was take over their mortgage payment of fifty dollars a month. It was a very generous offer, and we gratefully accepted. With John finishing college and me caring for our two young daughters, our money situation was stretched.

In the spring of 1971, my father's contract in Japan had ended. My parents, Bruce and Esther Shields, along with my younger siblings, Diane and Robert, returned home to San Diego. We had all been living together under one roof for several months while John finished his final weeks of graduate studies. John had been interviewing with various schools hoping to obtain a teaching job in the fall. Two families living under the same roof made the arrangement crowded and nerves were naturally on edge.

For the past two years, John had been working three part-time jobs while finishing his degree at San Diego State University. In 1962, John had signed to play professional baseball with the Dodger organization. As part of his signing bonus, his mother, Sue, had insisted that the organization would pay for his college education once his contract was over. It was a wise decision, and the $500 stipend sent each semester ensured that he remained in college. Even with the generous rental situation and the stipend, money had been tight. I held down a part-time job stocking sunglasses in small convenience stores, volunteered twice a week to teach physical education to seventh and eighth grade girls at Saint Patrick's School while raising our two daughters. Shauna would turn three in August and our baby girl, Tara, had turned one in June.

When John broached the idea of moving to Kenya, I looked at him in disbelief. I was angry. Lately, he had been away from the girls and me too much. 'You've been MIA for weeks! I know you've been working hard, and you're frustrated with our living situation, but it's been hard on me too. I have no car and two small babies to care for. It's been an adjustment for my parents as well after living in Japan for two years. I'm sure they'd like to have their home back.'

Upon graduating from San Diego State University in June 1970, we discussed completing John's post graduate work at California Western University to get his teaching degree. We knew attending a private university would be expensive, but the accelerated postgraduate program would allow John to begin teaching in the fall of 1971—a year earlier than the graduate program at San Diego State University. We decided to roll the dice. It was a gamble that would change the course of our lives for many years.

> *The nonprofit private university, known as Cal Western, is situated on a bluff overlooking the Pacific Ocean. The beautiful oceanfront campus in Point Loma is operated under the direction of William C. Rust. Rust's idea is to create a distinct global university under the title, United States International University (USIU). Rust's vision to install campuses worldwide is in development.*
>
> *To support his global vision, Rust eventually sells the expensive Point Loma property to Nazarene University and purchases less expensive land north of San Diego near Scripps Ranch with campus operations continuing there in 1973.*
>
> *In 1971, USIU is running three global campuses in London, Mexico City, and Nairobi. Today, the Nairobi campus is the only international campus still in operation and is known as United States International University Africa.*

'I know. I'm sorry, Linda. You know how much I love your parents, but two families living in the same house is a bit congested. You're right. I've been hiding out. But please, just hear me out. This could be the break for which we've been hoping. Cal Western is offering *us* a job! Of all the students in the postgraduate program, they approached me. The teaching market here is saturated at the moment. We may not get another offer.'

I knew he was right. If John didn't secure a teaching position, we would be stuck without a job, a place to rent, and our gamble to attend the more expensive private school would become a disaster.

'But Kenya seems so far, and I know nothing about Africa. Would it be safe for our girls? Where would we live?' I suddenly had wild notions of us living with our girls in mud huts among lions and leopards.

'Let's at least discuss it, Linda.'

I softened toward him. I knew how hard he had been working, and my biased attitude was based on my own selfish frustrations. I could tell he was extremely excited about this opportunity. 'Tell me about their offer.'

'Cal Western is becoming part of United States International University, a global university with projected campuses all over the world. They have invited me to teach Physical Education at one of their international schools in Nairobi. They've hired mostly single teachers but approached me to run their physical education department and coach three sports. We would be the only family invited out to Kenya this year.'

'When would we have to leave?'

'Well, that's the thing. USIU has chartered a plane to London leaving in mid-August. I have to let them know right away. If we accept, we'll have only four weeks to get our passports, visas, and the necessary inoculations to enter the country.'

The news blindsided me, but I promised myself to keep an open mind and at least hear him out. Finally, I said, 'Let's go inside the house and talk it over with Mom and Dad.'

John let out a sigh of relief and agreed. Having just returned from their two-year stint in Japan, I knew my parents would have helpful advice.

We walked into the house. My parents were sitting in the living room visiting with Mary Doris Hicks—a neighbor from the next street over. John discussed the university's job offer and Mary Doris got extremely excited.

'You know, National Geographic did a huge article on Kenya a while back. My husband, Larry, saves all those magazines. The article went on for pages and pages with beautiful photos—you know how National Geographic loves to do those in-depth features. I remember Nairobi as being a beautiful city. You guys should read it. I'll dash home and get it.' Mary Doris walked to the door and said, 'I'll be right back.'

My anxiety abated a little.

'What do you think, Mom?' I asked.

My mom looked at us and smiled. 'Our Japan experience was amazing, and…I might not be saying this if we hadn't lived out of the country for two years…but I think you should go.'

I was surprised at her quick response. 'You do?'

'I'll miss my granddaughters, but this is a great opportunity for you kids.'

'It's a wonderful chance to see another part of the world as a local resident and not just a tourist,' offered Dad. 'I agree with your mother.'

I looked over at John and sensed he was happy with the way things were going.

Dad continued, 'Shauna and Tara are so young; they'll go wherever you take them. When you visit a country as a tourist you see it from the eyes of a tourist. Living there, you'll have the opportunity to explore the country and learn the customs of the people. I know that living in Japan for two years gave us the time to explore the country in depth. We, of course will miss you, but I believe you definitely should go.'

We discussed the pros and cons of taking the job for the next thirty minutes. The one thing that stood out to me was my mother's words of wisdom when she said, 'If you decide to go, you should go with an open heart—with the thought that anytime you leave the United States—you're camping out.'

I laughed. 'What do you mean, Mom?' I was puzzled but knew my mother's Irish wit often had a humorous outlook on subjects.

'What I'm saying is try not to compare Africa to America. You might have situations where the electricity or the phones will go out. Things may not run as smoothly as they do here, but there'll be so many more blessings from your adventure that will last a lifetime.'

It turned out to be the best advice ever given to us, and I thought of it often over the course of our stay in Kenya.

Mary Doris and her husband returned with the article about Kenya. The *National Geographic* February 1969 spread spanned fifty-six pages and rendered an in-depth portrait of the newly formed republic, which had won its independence from Great Britian in December of 1963. The photos of the animals in the wild were magnificent, but the article highlighted the newly formed republic, under the leadership of President Jomo Kenyatta, as a developing democracy. Kenya's healthy economy had attracted blue-chip companies like Colgate-Palmolive, Union Carbide, Firestone, and Dole with the United States investing $100 million in Kenya since 1962.

The National Geographic article was the reassurance I needed to understand that Nairobi was a vibrant cosmopolitan city. We signed on with the university and within four weeks we were on a charter plane out of LAX to London, where we would stay at another USIU campus for a week to get the necessary visas and work permits to begin our life in Kenya. The only international travel I had done was to venture fourteen miles south of San Diego across the border to Tijuana, Mexico, to go clubbing or have my hair done. The days before our departure passed in a whirlwind of activity getting the necessary inoculations and passports for travel.

**Linda (Betsy) and John (Babe) passport photos
ages 25 and 27—1971.**

The day of our departure finally came. My head was spinning, wondering if I had forgotten anything as my father drove us north to LAX. Later, my mother wrote that she had found my Grandma Cassie's Rosary resting on a shelf in the refrigerator. Why I put it there, I will never know. It was a frenzied time. I laughed as I read her letter. Over the last weeks, I had wondered where the Rosary had gone, and was happy it had turned up.

As part of our contract, the university allowed us to ship via air one fifty-pound crate of personal goods to set up our house. I chose carefully, filling the container with kitchen items, pots and pans, towels, sheets, and eating utensils to supply our new dwelling. The single teachers did not choose as wisely and regretted having to purchase those items for their households.

John's Aunt Lucille worked for the Singer Sewing Company and suggested I buy a small sewing machine encased in a suitcase that was about the size of a woman's makeup case. It was very heavy. I lugged it on the plane pretending it to be nothing more than a carry-on toiletry case. That little Singer sewing machine paid for itself many times over. During our stay in Nairobi, I sewed all the girls' outfits. The majority of my clothes were fashioned with it—including a stylish two-piece bathing suit. I even made John a dress shirt and several pairs of shorts. I eventually had the little Singer shipped back home to San Diego.

It has been my only sewing machine for over fifty years. A few years ago, I took it into a Singer store to replace the band. The repairman told me, 'This little machine is the best product Singer ever made. It may be little but has the engine of a tractor. Hang on to it. They don't make them anymore.'

I smiled and nodded. He was so right.

✻ ✻ ✻ ✻ ✻

On August 14, 1971, we landed at Gatwick Airport, which is thirty-five miles north of central London, in the wee hours of the morning. A small bus had been secured in Luton to transport us south through the streets of London and onward to USIU campus in Ashdown, England. The bus driver kept telling us how lucky we were to see London this way as the traffic would become very congested in a few hours. He enjoyed pointing out things of interest. He took us past Big Ben, Westminster Abbey, and Covent Garden. I felt like Eliza Doolittle watching colorful flowers being unloaded by vendors and dustmen picking up trash. It was a wonderful way to see an awakening London for our first visit.

Because of our girls, we were given the entire back of the bus so they could stretch out on the long back seat and rest as we traveled to Ashdown. We covered them with our coats and the humming motion of the bus quickly lulled them to sleep.

It all seemed a bit surreal. Less than twenty-four hours before we had been sharing a home with my parents in San Diego. The reverential mood on the bus mirrored that of a church congregation. Along with the administrators and single teachers, we were all slightly in awe. John reached for my hand. No words were spoken. We looked at each other and smiled. My heart pumped with excitement, and I sensed John had similar feelings. We were at the starting block, ready to run the adventure of a lifetime.

From Luton, it took about two hours to reach Sussex, and the Ashdown Park campus, arriving at 7:30 AM. The countryside was lovely. The houses and farmland were so different from California. Green trees and colorful flowers grew in profusion. Herds of sheep and cattle grazed on the verdant grass of rolling hills. I knew we should have been tired, but the excitement of the moment masked any immediate need for sleep.

The Ashdown Park campus was something out of a fairytale.

The original estate circa 1693 comprised 3,563 acres, which included Pippingford Park, the Old Lodge, and the Army Training

Ground. Ashdown Park Mansion house was built in the 1800s. Located approximately thirty miles southeast of London in Sussex, the historic Ashdown Park estate was purchased by the Catholic Sisters of Notre Dame in 1919 as a suitable property for the purpose of training young novices. The Church of Our Lady and Saint Richard was built and consecrated in 1927. Over the years, several more buildings were added to the property. In 1971, the Chapel of Our Lady and Saint Richard is deconsecrated when Ashdown Park is sold to United States International University.

We were sequestered in a series of dorm rooms that were not in use. Before unpacking, we were invited to join a portion of the staff and students for breakfast in a large cafeteria.

The president of Nairobi International School, Doctor Hamilton, addressed the group, 'I suggest that we try to rest. Over the next week we will be busy procuring the necessary visas and work permits needed to reside in Kenya. I have booked us all on a bus tour of London later in the week. Any other free time might be used at your discretion to visit other areas near the city.'

We rested for most of the day. Later that afternoon, we bundled the girls in jackets and decided to stretch our legs. John and I were surprised at how cold and overcast it was. August in San Diego was always warm and sunny. The weather in Sussex that August was drizzly and cold, resembling something we might experience in winter.

We wandered about the grounds as the girls ran about smelling flowers and pointing at a rabbit in the distance. Several of the buildings seemed incredibly old. Everything was lush and green and so different from the dry summer months of San Diego. I was amazed to see the names of Norte Dame nuns on tombstones in a cemetery on the grounds. I made a mental note to write to my mom about it.

Eventually, we were approached by one of the gardeners. 'Are you part of the American group going to Kenya?'

'Yes, we are,' John replied.

'You folks should explore the outer grounds. They are really quite beautiful,' he offered as he pointed off in the distance.

John remarked, 'I saw a wooded area coming in this morning and thought we might take our girls for a walk. Is this part of your campus?'

'Oh yes. In fact, Ashdown Forest in East Sussex was the original inspiration for A.A. Milne's children's stories about *Winnie-the-Pooh*. In the early 1920s, Milne had a country home in Ashdown, which became the setting for The Hundred Acre Wood in his books. Milne was inspired by walks he took with his son, Christopher Robin, in Ashdown Forest. In fact, the Pooh character is based on a stuffed toy Milne had bought for Cristopher in Harrods department store.'

'Our girls love *Winnie-the Pooh* books. I believe the Walt Disney Company recently acquired the franchise from the author's estate. We've seen several animated movies based on the original books, and Pooh has joined Mickey and Minnie Mouse at Disneyland,' I offered.

The gardener looked down and gently kicked a stone which tumbled into a bush. 'Yeah, you Yanks sometimes have a way of hijacking a good thing. I guess money talks.'

We couldn't quite tell, but he seemed upset about Disney acquiring their national treasure, so John pointed and said, 'Over in that direction you said? Thanks for the tip.'

The gardener tipped his hat and shrugged his shoulders as we sheepishly headed off toward Ashdown Forest. The forest was lovely, and the girls delighted in seeing a deer in the mist drinking water from a pond.

The remainder of the week in England was spent going into London to procure visas. As a family, we enjoyed taking the train to the charming seashore town of Brighton. It was the first time I had ever seen rocks instead of sand lining the shore. I inwardly chuckled when I saw, in lieu of a hat, several older men wearing white handkerchiefs on their heads that had been knotted in all four corners to protect their heads from the sun. Our budget was tight, but John bought me an antique silver napkin ring in Brighton, which became the first of a lifelong collection of unusual antique napkin rings. On another day, we joined our group on a bus tour into London to visit The Tower of London, Westminster Abbey and other sites courtesy of Dr. Hamilton.

The week flew by and soon we were boarding a plane that would take us to Kenya.

Chapter 2:
1971 — Foreshadowing the Journey

As the plane banked for its final descent toward Nairobi's Embakasi Airport, I could see a large herd of dark-colored animals grazing on the dried yellow plains of the savanna, like tiny raisins scattered on a bed of oatmeal.

'What kind of animals are they, Mama?' asked our soon-to-be three-year-old daughter.

'I'm not sure, Shauna.'

A businessman from England in the next seat offered to help. 'Those look like they might be a herd of wildebeest to me.'

I smiled at the kind man and looked at my husband, John. I had pondered over the last weeks how we had ended up moving to Kenya. It had all happened so fast. Less than two months before we had been living in San Diego finishing John's postgraduate studies and preparing to begin his teaching career in San Diego. I glanced at our two young daughters and knew they were not old enough to understand that their lives had been torn from their grandparents and their extended family, but my mom was right. They seemed happy to be a part of it all. I never thought our paths would take us away from San Diego, but two events seemed to foreshadow where destiny might lead us.

John had enjoyed his post graduate work at Cal Western and loved his student teaching assignments. He came home excited after teaching a geography class at Grossmont High School, shortly before my parents were due to come home from Japan.

'I love my student teaching assignments! One of my master teachers told me I'll make a great physical education teacher and coach because I can project my voice.'

I nodded but thought it was an odd criterion to base one's teaching ability on the volume of voice projection. I decided to keep the thought to myself because I could see how excited he was to be practicing the craft he had worked so hard to complete.

'I'm teaching a unit on East Africa in my geography class. The area is fascinating. I don't know why, but I'm really drawn to that part of the world. Wouldn't it be great to visit there one day?'

'That would be nice, honey,' I responded with as much enthusiasm as I could muster, as he continued to relate the exciting events of his day. I mumbled some encouraging words as I sat folding cloth diapers and feeling I had little to share about the less than stirring events of my day.

The second event occurred a few weeks later on a rare night out with several of my girlfriends. We had gone to an all-girls Catholic school and had remained close over the years. However, being married and raising two babies, I was starting to realize I had less in common with my single girlfriends who were working, attending college, and hot on the dating scene.

One day, I received a call from my dear high school friend, Kate McManus, inviting me to come and hang out with her and three other friends from high school who were renting a house together in La Mesa.

'You have to come, Linda. We just finished final exams and we're celebrating with just a few friends at our place. Everyone misses you, so come,' implored Kate.

'I miss you girls too. I can't remember the last time I've done anything that didn't involve cooking or changing diapers I don't know, Kate. Money is tight with us at the moment, and I hate to ask John to watch the girls. He's been studying, student teaching, and working all these extra jobs while trying to graduate.'

'Ask him. We're planning to get together this Friday, and it's been ages since we've had a girls' night,' Kate said with unbridled enthusiasm.

John graciously agreed to watch our daughters so I could have a night out with the girls. I got directions and drove over to their rental house. It felt good to dress up and it was fun seeing everyone. However, I soon realized our lives had taken different directions. I had little in common with my single girlfriends. It's not that I was sad about the direction my life had taken. It simply was different. I decided to catch up with what was going on in their lives and make an early exit home to my family. An opportunity arose when a couple of the girls' boyfriends popped in for a visit to say hello.

"Are you sure you want to take off,' said Kate as she walked me outside to my car. 'The party is just getting started.' At that moment two handsome fellas got out of their car and walked over to where we stood.

Introductions were made. 'This is my friend, Nick Barkett, and my boyfriend, Sammy.'

With excitement Kate exclaimed, 'The three of us are planning a trip to Africa when school lets out this summer.'

'Africa?' I said thinking she might as well have said the moon. 'That's a long way to go.' It seemed so far from my world of reality. 'What part?' I asked. 'Africa is a big continent.'

'Oh, we don't know yet. Probably...somewhere in the north!' Kate offered as the boys nodded their heads in agreement.

'Wow. That should be amazing,' I fibbed.

As I drove home, I realized my life, as a wife and a mother, was far different from my single girlfriends, who had little no about children. I was a little jealous and a little bewildered as I thought about Kate, the boyfriend Sammy, and the friend Nick and their loosely planned venture to visit Africa. Yet another part of me was thinking they were out of their minds, because *somewhere* in Africa would be one of the last places on earth to which I would want to travel.

As we all weave the tapestry of our lives, I sense that events have a way of working out in the manner in which they are intended. I have often reflected on those two foreshadowing occasions. Perhaps I was being prepared for a grander scheme which I was meant to experience.

Three months later, I found *myself* flying into Kenya and reflecting om those the two curious events with my husband John and my friend Kate.

During our second year in Kenya, we received a beautiful wedding photo from Kate. The boyfriend, Sammy, had faded into oblivion. Kate and Nick's friendship blossomed into love, and they were married in 1972. They have been married for over fifty years, have three boys, and seven grandchildren. The trip to *somewhere* in Africa never materialized.

* * * * * *

We landed on the tarmac in Nairobi and descended the steps of the plane into the warm equatorial sun. Airport workers escorted us across the runway and into a small terminal. We were tired, and it took an eternity to collect our luggage and be processed to enter the country as residents with work visas.

Several teachers from Nairobi International School had come to escort Dr. Hamilton, his wife, Harriet, and about a dozen of us who would begin teaching at the elementary or secondary levels of the school we had come to call NIS. We were lucky to ride to the campus with a delightful American couple, Ramon and Pat Stade. Ramon was the principal of the school, and Pat worked in the office. They had two young boys. Pat became a lifeline to me and imparted wonderful information on everything a housewife needed to survive in Nairobi. Within days, she drove me into the city, showing me all the best shops to buy deli meats and green groceries. She treated me to my first ever curry at her favorite restaurant. I wasn't an immediate fan, but soon came to love the spicy delicacies that substituted for our missing Mexican cuisine.

We were given accommodations at the school's dorm until we could find a place to rent. Lots of the teachers stopped by to tell us, and sometimes *frighten* us, with tales of the local tribes harassing farms in an effort to win their independence just six years before.

Mau Mau warriors were a rebellious wing of the native population who sought political freedom and representation in Kenya's government from Britain. Many native Kenyans resented the annexation of most of the richest agricultural areas in Kenya. Beginning in the early nineteen hundreds, the British government eventually seized seven million square miles of fertile land. The British needed cheap labor to work the land, which the government acquired often through force or human necessity. The Mau Mau rebels did not possess much in the way of artillery and heavy weaponry so most of the attacks against Kenya loyalist and British colonialists were perpetrated at night in a gorilla-style fashion. The movement began in 1952 and continued to 1960. Eventually Kenya won its independence and became a republic in December 1963, electing Jomo Kenyatta as its first president.

Chapter 3:
1971-1972 — The Drums of Thika

One might say we arrived in Kenya on a wing and a prayer—young, naive, and confident that things would work out *just fine*. Unfortunately, we were mistaken. We possessed a mere seven hundred dollars as the sum total of our funds for starting a new life in Africa. With this, we had to buy a used car and procure living accommodations. What were we thinking! Most of the single teachers banded together and rented places in a suburb of Nairobi called Westlands. It was near Nairobi International School and made for an easy commute. We searched the want ads in the *Daily Nation* and the *East African Standard* for houses to rent and used cars for sale.

We got lucky, or so we thought, and purchased an old green Volkswagen bus that had been put out to pasture by the East Africa Phone Company. It was in our price range, and we thought it would be perfect for going on safari. Unfortunately, it ended up being a poor investment. Something went wrong with it every other month.

As for housing, there was nothing to rent around the city of Nairobi in our price range, so we widened our search in the farming country outside the city. We found a Kikuyu man named Mr. Guthega who lived in an area northeast of Nairobi called Thika. Before Kenya's independence, Thika was settled as a farming community by white European colonials. Huge coffee plantations and other crops grew on large plots of land

and reflected what must have been genteel country living in British colonial Kenya. In 1971, the area consisted of a mixture of European expatriates, who chose to stay after Kenya's independence, and a new evolving upper-class group of Kenyans consisting mostly of the Kikuyu ethnic tribe.

Mr. Guthega owned a large coffee plantation and was a personal friend of Kenya's first and current president, Jomo Kenyatta. Besides coffee, he grew potatoes and other vegetables, raised chickens, cattle, and sheep, and ran a small efficient dairy. He lived with his wife and children in an attractive house near the entrance to his farm. We met him at his house, and he drove us to another section of his property where two other houses were situated. He offered to rent us a small stone guest cottage set apart from a large manor house, which he had recently rented to a Nigerian diplomat, his wife, and young daughter.

The little stone cottage was charming. It was a single story with a high-pitched roof and two small dormer windows in the attic, which gave it an English country feel. The cottage possessed two bedrooms, a small kitchen, equipped with a little refrigerator and stove, and a small round table and chairs in the dining area adjoining the kitchen. One small bathroom, and a decent-sized living area with a fireplace completed the layout of the cottage. It was sparsely furnished, but most of the places we had considered had been unfurnished. The front of the house had a large lawn with several mature shade trees. A beautiful bottle brush tree and an assortment of colorful flowers grew all around the cottage. To one side of the house was an area suitable for planting a good-sized vegetable garden. The back section of the cottage had a cement patio permanently stained with the rich red soil of Kenya. A separate little stone house behind the kitchen had been built as living quarters for a house servant.

Off to the side of the servant's building was a large empty chicken coop. Mr. Guthega said, 'I will give you a few chickens if you take the house.' I wondered, *This area is away from the city, maybe he is having difficulty renting this property...or is there something else?*

I could see that John was excited about living in the country. John turned to Shauna and said, 'I can make you girls a swing from the branch of this big oak tree.'

Shauna jumped up and down and said, 'Oh yes, Daddy. Make us a swing.'

As we continued our tour of the area, I could hear the pleasant sound of water splashing in the distance. I asked Mr. Guthega about it.

'Let me give you an expanded tour of the property.' We walked down a sloping dirt road that led to a large stone house with manicured grounds. The sound of water grew louder.

'Located beyond these trees is the larger house that I have rented to a Nigerian diplomat and his family.' He pointed to a beautiful manor house surrounded by large trees. 'But come follow me. This area of my property is quite beautiful. It has a pretty waterfall. I will show it to you.'

We walked along a dirt road past the manor house, where a small creek flowed at the bottom of a slope. The area was lush with trees, shrubs, and flowers near the water's edge. A small waterfall danced off of rocks and fed into the little creek.

'This water is lazy at the moment, but it will grow when the rainy season comes.' Mr. Guthega beamed. 'It has been told to me that an early Tarzan movie from the thirties was once filmed here, but I am not sure if this is true.'

'The area is enchanting, and its jungle-feel seems as though it might have been a fine location to film a Tarzan movie,' I offered.

Walking back toward the guest cottage, Mr. Guthega pointed out an area of huts directly across the dirt road from the cottage. The African encampment held about fifteen small huts made from tree branches and packed together with fine red Kenya soil. The huts were covered with thatched roofs. The encampment housed the men, women and children who worked on Mr. Guthega's farm. Several small naked children played in the dirt. He walked us over and addressed his workers in Swahili. He pointed us out to them. When he was finished, he walked over to where we stood near the dirt road.

'This settlement is for my workers who help on my farm. I told them you might be renting the guest cottage. They will not give you trouble, so you should not worry about them.'

The cottage was in our price range, and we were on a deadline. NIS would soon be in session, and we had to vacate the dorm to make way for the influx of boarding students attending the college portion of the campus. We shook hands on the deal and agreed that we would move in on the following Saturday afternoon and would settle our first month's rent at that time. However, we had a problem.

After purchasing our Volkswagen bus, we didn't have enough money to rent the cottage. Later that afternoon, John approached Dr. Hamilton at the school, and he graciously gave us an advance on our first paycheck. John was never one to worry about the tiny details in life. I was the worrier in our family. He always felt things would work out in the end. John was usually right.

The following Saturday afternoon, we vacated the dorm and made the thirty-minute drive to Thika and the little stone cottage. Our only belongings consisted of the items in our suitcases, a few groceries, and the fifty pounds of household supplies that had been shipped by air to the school. As arranged, Mr. Guthega met us at the cottage to give us our keys. A tall imposing African man stood next to him. His skin was the color of onyx, which seemed to shine in the daylight. The man had an imposing scar on the left side of his face. Mr. Guthega turned and introduced us to him.

'This man is named Francis. He will be your askari.'

We looked confused. Mr. Guthega explained. 'He is an askari—in Swahili askari means policeman or night watchman—Francis will look after you.' Francis wore a long black military-style woolen coat, which fell almost to his ankles. He was very tall and carried a flashlight and a large machete, which the Kenyans call a *panga*. I wondered how Francis had gotten his scar. At the time, I became a little unsettled about needing a watchman, but we grew to appreciate Francis in the months to come.

Often when we pulled into our driveway in the evening, we were surprised when Francis, who blended into the night so well, would step out of dark shadows and greet us with, '*Jambo memsahib. Jambo bwana. Hujambo?*' This greeting meant;

Hello and how do you do? After recovering from being startled, we would politely answer, '*Sijambo*, or *Habari sana*, Francis,' meaning; it is well with us. At this point Francis would invariably try to engage us in conversation. I believe Francis was very lonely as an askari and enjoyed passing the time with small talk to ease the solitude of his job.

We soon discovered that living in the country of Kenya was vastly different from living in a modern city like San Diego. In the city, even on a moonless night, we take ambient light for granted—the corner streetlamp, a lighted stop signal, the porch light from your neighbor's home, or the headlights from a nearby car. Living in the country, we had no close neighbors, and the manor house was fifty yards away and camouflaged by its surrounding trees. Moonless nights in Thika were as dark as a murky cave. The only sound might be the barking of a distant dog, or the growl of a feral cat.

After a busy day arranging our meager supplies in the cottage and making the beds, we had a light supper and settled in for the evening. Over the course of our time in Kenya, I came to enjoy being just one hundred miles south of the equator. It always got dark in or around 7:00 PM—give or take five minutes. This made for an adaptable schedule when raising young children. We bathed and put our girls down for the night at seven.

John and I settled ourselves in the lounge on the couch and armchair that had come with the house. We had been so busy arranging our things that we had not thought to gather wood to start a cozy fire in the brick fireplace. With no television or radio and little to no outside light, we suddenly realized how alone we were in the country. We had not yet arranged to have our phone service connected. It became unnervingly quiet, so we decided to pass the time reading.

I looked up from my book and said, 'John, it just occurred to me that *no one* from the school knows where we are. I hope we haven't made a mistake renting a house so far out in the country. Our phone is not set up yet, and I just realized that we live in the middle of a coffee plantation in a house with no street name off a dirt road.'

'I know, Linda. I thought of that too. I'll admit living so far out in the country is not exactly ideal, but I'm sure it'll be fine. Try and focus on your book.' We continued to read for another thirty minutes.

Deathly silence once again enveloped the room like a cold fog, until suddenly, we heard the sound of a drum beating in the distance. I waited, thinking it would stop. The drum began as a solo instrument, but soon other drums joined in, and the sound intensified.

I looked over at my husband, who had stopped reading his book and was staring off in the distance toward the sound. 'John, what in the hell is that?'

'I don't know, but I'm not going outside to look. I hope Francis, is nearby.' I looked across the room at John and could tell he was even a bit shaken. Neither of us continued to read.

We had only been in Kenya for two weeks, and I immediately began to question why we had rented a house outside the city. We knew little about the customs and practices of the local people. When we first arrived, several teachers had loved telling us stories about how the Mau Mau uprising had contributed to Kenya's independence a mere seven years before. At the time, it had made me a little annoyed believing they took delight in trying to scare us. These memories flooded my thoughts as we quietly sat in the cottage.

We continued to listen to the steady rhythm of drums in the distance. My mind vividly went to those Saturday afternoon black and white matinee features on television. The old B-rated movies that I had often watched with my best friend, Terry, when we were young.

You know, the ones with white hunters, like Clark Gable or Robert Mitchum, on a jungle safari in Africa. I shared my memories of these old movies with John and could see that his imagination was as heightened as mine.

'How did storylines usually end in these tales?'

'I remember the plots of these movies often ran along similar storylines—when the *native* drums stopped beating—the white men usually got into trouble.'

'That's not comforting, Linda!'

The noise indicated that more people had joined in and were now chanting to the rhythm of the drums.

'Oh, God,' I whispered, 'maybe that's why Mr. Guthega hired Francis to guard our cottage.'

John looked over at me and uttered, 'I'm sure it's fine,' in a voice that did nothing to alleviate my fear.

We continued to listen for another twenty minutes until John said, 'Oh, what the hell.' He looked at his watch and said, 'It's eight o'clock. There's nothing we can do. Let's just go to bed.'

It took us a long time to fall asleep, but finally we drifted off to the rhythm of drums beating steadily in the distance.

We awoke the next morning with our girls clamoring over the side of our bed. It was a clear sunny day and the only sound we heard was that of birds chirping in a bottlebrush tree outside our bedroom window. John leaned over and wryly said, 'We made it.'

'That's not funny.' But he was right. Things did look a lot brighter in the morning sun.

Later that morning, Mr. Guthega came by with a dozen eggs and two hens in a wooden crate.

'I came to see how you are settling in,' he said as we greeted him on the cement patio by the back door.

John casually mentioned, 'Yes, everything's fine. We were wondering though. Last night we heard the sound of drums beating in the distance. Any idea what that might be about?'

Mr. Guthega let out a belly laugh. 'Oh, I'm sorry if this may have concerned you. I should have remembered to tell you. Every Saturday night, my workers like to rejoice after working all week. They have a little *ngoma*...a celebration with drums and dancing. It is nothing. You should not worry about it. Francis, your askari, is here to watch over you.'

We both waved our hands in the air—brushing away his explanation as if it were an annoying fly.

'Of course, of course, that's exactly what we both thought,' said John.

We lived in that little stone cottage for one year and every Saturday night we looked at each other and smiled a little, as we listened to the drums of Thika beating in the distance.

* * * * * *

Front and rear views of our stone cottage in Thika

And so, our lives began in Kenya. We soon settled into country life. Mr. Guthega helped us hire a Kikuyu house-girl named Rose. True to his word, John built a swing for the girls and hung it from the large oak tree. Shortly after renting the cottage a kitten, the girls named Posie and a yellow labrador puppy the girls named Peaches, joined the chickens as part of our family. Peaches was a beautiful lab that had been given to us by one of the teachers at NIS. Peaches had been the unfortunate offspring of inbreeding, and the family felt, in good conscience, they couldn't sell her. She was a great dog and bore dozens of mixed-breed pups during our five-year stay in Kenya.

We had an unusual relationship with our indigenous neighbors. They kept to their traditions, and we followed ours. Other than waving from their village across the road, we rarely interacted. Our three-year-old daughter, Shauna, occasionally wandered over to hang out with the *mtotos*—the children of the workers. All was well, but from time to time, we noticed that things had a way of going missing. One day, I could not find Peaches' metal water bowl, which I kept near the back door on the patio.

I asked Rose if she had seen it. 'I saw this bowl yesterday, Memsahib, as I removed the washing from the clothesline in the afternoon. I do not know where it has gone to.'

I walked over to where Shauna was swinging on the tree swing. 'Shauna, have you seen the dog bowl? Rose said it was on the patio yesterday afternoon.'

Without saying a word, our three-year-old daughter jumped off the swing and took off running in the direction of the Kikuyu village. I watched as she ran in and out of several of the huts. She eventually came darting across the road with the missing dog bowl in her hands.

'Where did you find it?'

'I looked until I found it underneath a bed in one of the little huts. There was an old lady sitting inside smoking a pipe, but she didn't say anything to me. I just grabbed it and ran home.'

'Did anyone else say anything or try to stop you?'

'No. The old lady in the little hut just looked at me.'

Later that evening, as I relayed the story to John, I said, 'Not only is our little girl brave, but I have a feeling she will always have a strong moral compass as to what is right and wrong.'

To this day, my daughter, Shauna, has lived her life with an embedded sense of what is right and what is wrong. It's an endearing trait that I knew she had even at three.

* * * * * *

The iron red soil on the Kenyan plateau around Nairobi is rich in nutrients. I often felt one could casually drop a seed in the ground and a beautiful, lush plant would burst forth. NIS had yet to pay us for our housing allowance and moving expenses. Money was extremely tight. We decided it would be wise to grow a *shamba*—a garden to help with expenses. Plus, John felt it would give me something to fill my time while he was at school. We tilled the rich red soil and planted a variety of vegetables—tomatoes, onions, potatoes, squash, carrots, green beans, peppers, pumpkins, and corn. It was a fairly large garden, and we were pleased with our forward thinking. John was right. The garden helped fill my days living alone in the country, and I nurtured it as one might nurture a young child.

One evening after John returned from NIS, I announced that I thought one of our plants looked like it might be ready for harvesting. We walked out for an inspection and agreed that the zucchini squash was definitely ready for picking. I was excited and got out the only recipe book I had chosen to bring to Kenya, a *Better Homes and Garden Cookbook*, which I received as a wedding gift and was a *must have* for every young bride in America at that time. That evening, I scanned it looking for potential recipes.

The next morning, I waved John off to school, gathered my garden tools, and headed over to our *shamba* with my daughters, ready to reap the rewards of our labor. I stopped cold. Half the zucchini squash appeared to have vanished. At first, I wondered if it was my imagination harboring a more grandiose idea of my skill as a farmer. But the pattern of missing produce continued to plague us at various times of our harvests. A crop of tomatoes or peppers would ripen, but before we could reap its full benefits, half of our crop would turn up missing.

The only crop we were able to fully harvest was our stalks of corn. Kenyans know nothing of what we call sweet corn. They eat larger ears of corn, which we know as maize. In America, this variety of field corn is mostly used as feed for animals. This larger variety of maize is less sweet and a little tough. It was immensely popular with the locals. On visits into the city, I had seen local vendors roasting cobs of maize over coals on street corners for sale. Grain from the maize was also used as a stiff porridge, called posho that was often paired with cabbage. Leftover porridge was also pressed into a snowball that workers would eat cold for lunch. I suspected our Kikuyu neighbors or Francis never pilfered the corn from our garden because they must have thought it had not yet reached maturity. Our bountiful crop of corn was our finest success.

* * * * * *

Living in the country was a challenge for me. I was incredibly lonely and missed my family. The Kikuyu girl Mr. Guthega had sent over to assist me with the duties of the house and help care for our girls was young and not much company for me. Rose was still in her teens, and we had little in common. I once congratulated her on speaking two languages—English and Swahili and the advantages it afforded.

She said, 'Yes Memsahib, but you also speak two languages.'

'What two languages do you think I speak, Rose?'

'You speak English and American.'

I choked back a laugh and said, 'Rose, in America, English is the official language.'

She looked confused so I tried to explain. 'Like Kenya, America was once a British colony, and we also won our independence and became a republic. Most people in America speak English because our forefathers were English.'

Rose said, 'Then we have much in common.'

Because I was lonely, I filled my days in the country sewing on my little Singer sewing machine, gardening, playing my guitar, cooking, baking bread and experimenting with all sorts of desserts. Years later, John told me that our year in Thika was one of the happiest times in his life.

When I asked him why, he told me, 'Every day, when I got home from teaching and coaching you greeted me with a Tusker beer from a frosty mug you kept chilled in the freezer. You often treated the family to a new recipe you had tried that day. You made homemade bread and delicious desserts. But mostly, I always knew that my family would be waiting to welcome me home in our little cottage.'

I laughed. 'That's because being so bored and lonely, I had to find something creative to fill my days. In order to stay active and creative, I made countless recipes from my *Better Homes and Garden Cookbook.*'

* * * * * *

In the course of my interactions with the indigenous people of Kenya, I came to understand they are extremely forthright. Most Americans and British will cover an awkward encounter with the nuance of a polite comment to mask what they *really* feel on a subject. That is not the case with an African, as I learned the hard way.

In Kenya, tropical fruits like pineapples, mangoes, papayas, and bananas were reasonably priced. Apples, pears, and grapes were imported items and much more expensive. I got it into my head that I wanted to make an apple pie for John's dinner. I knew it would be an extravagant and costly dessert. All day, I fussed over the crust and made the filling just as I had seen my mother do. The pie filled the house with the sweet aroma of cinnamon as it baked, and I gazed at its beauty while it cooled by the open window on the kitchen counter. My joy continued with the array of compliments from my family around the dinner table. I was enormously proud, so after Rose and I cleaned the kitchen, I decided to send Rose off to her living quarters with a slice of the treasured treat.

The next day I waited for her to compliment me on the pie, but she went about her chores never mentioning it. When I could stand it no longer, I asked, 'Rose, how did you like my apple pie?'

She wrinkled her nose, shook her head, and said, 'I did not like this pie, Memsahib.'

I was crushed. 'Oh,' I said, trying not to look crestfallen. 'Why didn't you like the pie?'

Rose puckered her face in distaste. 'This pie was too sweet! I could not eat it!'

At first, I was irritated because the pie was expensive to make. I felt she had not appreciated my effort and generosity in sharing it with her. Later, when I thought more on the subject, I came to realize she had probably never eaten a sugary fruit pie and maybe she was expecting it to taste like the savory meat-filled pies so enjoyed by the English or East Indians. As I lay in bed that night, I sulked and thought *she could have lied and just pretended to like it.*

Over time, I came to learn that the nuanced perception a person in Western society will use to soften a situation is not in the African's way of thinking. And in truth, the African way is healthier.

Like me, I think our askari, Francis, was very lonely. He loved to corner us for a chat when we drove home in the evening. John was much more gracious about talking with him than I was, as I hustled the girls in the house for bedtime. One night Francis knocked on our kitchen door. When I opened it, he was holding a live chicken under his arm.

He asked, 'Is bwana John at home, Memsahib?'

'Yes, Francis, wait here and I'll get him.' John walked out to the patio to talk to him. About thirty minutes later, he entered the house.

I asked him, 'What was that about?'

'Francis was so pleased to have gotten to know us, he wanted to give us a chicken. I put it in the coop with the other chickens. Francis says the chicken doesn't lay eggs but would make a fine dinner for us.'

I looked at John in horror. 'Are you going to kill the chicken?

John looked at me and shrugged. 'I don't know. My Aunt Lucille used to think nothing of ringing a chicken's neck on their farm. I'm not sure if I'll do it. Right now, it's in the chicken coop. We'll deal with it tomorrow.'

Months went by. We continued to feed the chickens with scraps from our garden and chicken feed. Every once in a while, Francis would ask us, 'Bwana, when are you going to cook the chicken?'

'Soon, Francis,' John offered. 'We are waiting for the right time.'

One morning we woke up to a completely empty chicken coop. All the chickens had gone missing in the night. We wondered if Francis had taken the chickens—because we obviously didn't appreciate having a fine chicken dinner, or they had gone the way of our vegetables to our Kikuyu neighbors across the road.

No one, especially us, was talking about the missing chickens. In truth, we were actually relieved. John was dreading the day he would have to wring the chicken's neck, and I was not looking forward to plucking the feathers. We did miss the eggs.

Chapter 4:
November 1971 — Safari to Aberdare National Park

November arrived. The short rains had finished, and the sun continued to beat down on the equator. Because the city of Nairobi rests five thousand feet above sea level, the climate is similar to San Diego, which is cooled by the Alaskan current from the north for those lucky enough to live within ten miles of the coast. By a similar coincidence, the heat of the equatorial sun is offset by the 5,000-foot elevation of Nairobi, which sits on a plateau. The lower savanna regions were typically hot and dry in the summer and hot and humid at the coast. We felt very much at home living in the high elevation of Nairobi, which tempers the mood of the equatorial sun.

We had gradually settled into country life for two months, with both of us finding a rhythm that filled our time. John loved his job teaching physical education to the high school students at NIS. He said it was a dream job. The students who attended the school were primarily the children of American and European diplomats. Others came from families who were working at one of the large American industrial businesses. The school catered to students wanting to pursue a higher college education in America. The United States had recently invested millions in the newly formed republic. Companies like Dole and Firestone employed Americans from all over the U.S. The school had an agreement with the government to allow a small percentage of Kenyan students to attend on a scholarship basis. The students from Great Britain attended one of the many private English schools that had been established during the colonial period.

One day John came home from teaching and told me he had grown fond of a sophomore student named Chris Bane, who shared his love of fishing. 'He's a great kid, Linda. He's only fifteen but he has the maturity of someone much older.'

'That seems to be a common theme with many of your students,' I offered as I poured him a bottle of Tusker beer into the icy mug I had pulled from the freezer.

'I know. My students are very sophisticated. I assume it's because they have traveled abroad with their parents. I know I wasn't as self-assured when I was that age. This kid is really special. How would you like to go camping in Aberdare National Park?'

'With what? We don't have any camping gear.'

'That's no problem. Chris and his family are avid outdoorsmen. We've been swapping fishing stories. I told him about fly fishing with your Uncle Bob in the Sierra Nevada Mountains last year. He said that he knows of a stream in the Aberdare Mountains where he caught small fingerling trout with his father.'

'What brings Chris and his family to Kenya?'

'I'm not exactly sure. I know his dad does something at the American Embassy. I told him we didn't have much in the way of camping gear, but he said his parents have…cots, tents, a Coleman stove…cooking supplies…sleeping bags…lanterns.

Chris says his family has everything. He's going to talk to them tonight.'

'That's thoughtful of him and his parents. That is, if they agree to let him come with us.'

'The place he wants to show us sounds amazing, and it's not that far from here. He said we could leave on a Friday after school, stay two nights and return on Sunday. Chris said there's a prime camping site in the Aberdare Mountains next to a creek with rainbow trout. He said elephants roam the area even though it's about seven thousand feet in elevation. We have been itching to see some of the country and this would be a terrific opportunity.'

'That's very generous considering we don't really know this family. Perhaps we should call them.'

'You're right and we will.'

I could see that John was extremely excited to venture out on our first safari. We both were eager to explore the country.

'When would we go?'

'Chris said he would connect with his folks and let me know tomorrow.'

The following Friday we picked Chris up from his home, packed the camping gear in our old green Kombi bus and headed out on our first safari. The quickest way to the Aberdare Mountains would have been through the town of Nyeri, but John wanted to finally see the Great Rift Valley.

The East African Rift Valley is part of the
ancient Great Rift Valley, which stretches
three thousand seven hundred miles south

from Syria to Mozambique and averages 30 to 40 miles in width. When violent subterranean forces tore apart the earth's crust, the earth's continental plates split apart causing the land to sink and create a huge depression called a rift. Today, the valley features volcanoes, hot springs, geysers, lakes, and frequent earthquakes. The East African Rift continues to split the continent of Africa in two. Several rift lakes dot the valley floor. These alkali-rich soda lakes like Lake Nakuru are home to tilapia fish and multitudes of pink flamingoes. These ancient lakes were formed as fresh water flooded and settled into the lower regions of the valley and became soda lakes. Important paleoanthropological discoveries have been uncovered in the East African Rift and it has often been called the cradle of humanity. A 1.5-million-year-old skeleton called Turkana Boy was unearthed in the northern part of the East African Rift Valley.

We left Nairobi after school on Friday and set out toward the west and finally came to the escarpment of the Rift Valley. We pulled off the road to an area offering drivers a great panoramic viewpoint of the valley. The view was stunning, and the steep drop gave a clear picture of the ancient rift running north and south. Chris pointed out a cone-shaped mountain.

'That's Mount Longonot. It was formed from a volcano. Can you see where the volcano blew its top, Shauna?' asked Chris.

Already I could see what a nice young man Chris was, and it was thoughtful of him to include Shauna in our conversation. Soon we were weaving our way down the steep escarpment, with the sides of the rift steadily dropping to the valley floor.

Off to the right, Chris pointed to a small chapel nestled against the eastern side of the lower escarpment. 'During WWII British soldiers allowed the Italian prisoners of war to build the Catholic chapel in 1942. The prisoners were conscripted to build the dangerous road down the escarpment and wanted to erect a place of worship.'

I thought the little chapel was charming. The sandstone-colored bricks and red tile roof looked like a landscape painting in Tuscany and must have reminded the prisoners of home. We pulled the Volkswagen bus off the side of the road, parked near its entrance, and stepped inside the cool interior of the little chapel for a few minutes to kneel and say a prayer.

**Chapel built against the escarpment
by Italian prisoners of war**

Continuing on the tarmac road led us to the bottom of the valley floor. The landscape had changed. The short rains had ended in October, with the weather being warm but not hot. The arid valley was scattered with a variety of trees and shrubs. Thorn trees dotted the area. We could see small herds of zebra, giraffe, and impala on each side of the road.

We drove until we arrived at Lake Naivasha. Chris told us that there was an old lodge built when Kenya was still a colony. We left the main road and turned right to a smaller road that would take us into the western entrance of Aberdare Game

Reserve. As we climbed up the mountain, the dry valley gave way to lush green trees and the temperature grew cooler.

'The top of the mountains can reach as high as nine thousand feet, but we will camp at about seven thousand feet. The weather will be beautiful in the day, but the temperature will become pretty cold at night,' offered Chris.

As we continued to climb in elevation, the lush green forest gave way to sparse-looking trees and shrubbery and soon the higher altitude put us into the tundra. We set up camp near a beautiful clear creek that was about thirty yards wide, and Chris and John decided to fish before it got too dark. Following the creek, I took the girls for a short walk and was surprised to see it spill over the side of a cliff into a waterfall, which cascaded down the side of the mountain. I made a mental note to never let the girls out of my sight. Herds of mountain elephants roamed the area, but other than spotting their occasional cylinder-shaped droppings, they stayed a safe distance from our camp.

The camping trip was fun. John was particularly relaxed, and I finally knew we had made the right decision to move to East Africa. The boys caught six or seven trout that were about nine inches in length, which we cooked for dinner. Chris continued to amaze us as a young man wise beyond his fifteen years. He shared stories about his family and the various places they had lived through his dad's job working for the American government. The weekend getaway ended all too soon and we were sad to break camp.

We packed our camping gear and loaded ourselves into the old green bus to head back to Nairobi. John turned the key but could not get the engine to turn over. We were only mildly concerned at this point. One of John's part-time jobs while attending college was working for Standard Oil at a Chevron station. He had a cursory knowledge of how an engine worked.

John opened the back of the bus to peer into where the engine resided. He tried adjusting wires and cables to no avail. Hours passed and we were getting a little worried, when suddenly to our relief two national park rangers came by in their Range Rover and offered to tow us down to Nyeri. We felt incredibly lucky at that moment. The park rangers hitched our bus to their rover with a thick rope and we began the descent down the mountain. In minutes, we were coughing from the dust spraying into our car from the tow. Every time we came to a steeper part of the road, the rangers would get out and remove the rope, allowing us to coast down the hill, giving us a respite from the thick dust flowing into the bus. This went on for what seemed to be hours, but I'm sure it was only my imagination.

We finally arrived in the town of Nyeri and were dropped off at the Outspan Hotel. This posh tourist establishment was built as a grandiose hotel for guests and tourists to be taken by bus for an overnight visit to another lodge called Treetops. Built on stilts, Treetops Lodge was designed to allow tourists to get up close with elephants and other wildlife who are coaxed into the area with salt licks and watering holes.

The Outspan Hotel in Nyeri, Kenya was built on existing farm in the 1920s by Eric Sherbrooke Walker, who purchased sixty-nine

acres of Crown Land. The beautiful hotel opened in 1928 with forty-five rooms, and 20 acres of gardens which afforded a stunning view of the Aberdare Range and Mount Kenya. The Outspan Hotel served as an adjunct facility which could be used to take guests and tourists for an overnight stay at its sister facility, the Treetops Hotel. Built into the tops of trees near a watering hole, the unique hotel provided an excellent opportunity for viewing local animals. In 1952, young Princess Elizabeth and Prince Philip were visiting Treetops when she received word that her father, King George VI, had suddenly passed away, and she had ascended to the throne as queen of England. That event cemented the popularity of the Outspan Hotel and Treetops and scores of international tourists became eager to visit it. The Treetops Hotel closed in 2021 when the tourism rate declined, due to the COVID-19 pandemic.

We walked into the lobby of the hotel not realizing how filthy we were from camping and the dusty ride down the mountain. Our camping clothes were wrinkled, and our bodies and hair were caked with a layer of fine Kenya dirt.

As we made our way to the reception desk, we heard the murmurings of several British and other tourists, in crisp new safari gear, as they stared at us in wide-eyed horror. Guests began clearing a wide path to let us through to the desk. I felt like we were Israelites led by Moses as he parted the Red Sea.

A handsome Kikuyu man looked up from his ledger and stared at us. 'Might I assist you, bwana?'

John explained our situation. 'Yes, our car broke down while camping in the Aberdare Mountains and park rangers towed us here. I would like a large room with a fireplace for me and my family for one night. Can you accommodate us?'

The receptionist peered at John from head to torso. 'I will presume you do not have a reservation, bwana?'

'No, and we'll only be staying for one night if we can get our car repaired tomorrow.'

The receptionist checked his book and said he had a room on the lower floor.

'I will also need to use your phone to call someone in Nairobi to explain our situation.'

The man behind the desk allowed John to call Chris' father, Howard, who told us not to worry. John also asked him if he might let Nairobi International School know that he would need a substitute teacher for Monday. When that was taken care of John asked where he might find a good mechanic.

'Ah, bwana, there is but one mechanic in town, but you will have to wait and call them in the morning. I do not believe they are open on Sunday. It is fairly close, and they should be able to tow your car from the parking lot. Dinner is included with your stay.' He looked at John and frowned. Do you have other clothes? You cannot go to dinner as you are.'

'We'll do the best we can.'

A bellman showed us to our room, and we all took turns taking a shower. The room consisted of one king-size bed. It was decided that John the girls and I would share it. This left us wondering about a bed for Chris. John and Chris got creative and pushed two overstuffed chairs together and Chris spent the night there.

I was exhausted from the entire experience and let Chris and John go to dinner while I stayed back and rested with the girls. John brought the girls cheese and crackers from the van. Food was the furthest thing from my mind.

I lay in bed feeling a little concerned. We were in charge of a young man we hardly knew. I worried that Chris' parents might think we weren't responsible and might regret allowing their son to go camping with us.

The next morning John got the mechanics to tow the old green bus to the garage and they replaced the carburetor. On Monday afternoon we drove toward Nairobi.

We made it safely back to Nairobi and dropped Chris and the camping gear at his parents' home. In the end, we need not have been concerned. Chris' parents were very understanding and told us that things like this often happened in Kenya. We didn't realize it at the time, but that camping trip set in motion a series of events which would change our lives over the next four years. The trip with Chris set us on a journey to become undercover spies for the CIA.

Chapter 5:
1971-72 Nairobi International School

Every once in a while, I was called upon to be a substitute teacher at the elementary or secondary portions of NIS. I looked forward to these days. Rose would watch the girls, and I got to wear a dress or a pantsuit and drive into the school with John. The stipend was meager—one hundred shillings—just fourteen dollars a day, but I didn't care. I was finally meeting people and making friends.

Nairobi International School was situated next to a large coffee plantation just northwest of a suburb of Nairobi called Westlands. In the seventies, the little village of Westlands had a small supermarket, a greengrocer, and a meat market. A petrol station and a few other small shops, which lined the street, completed the business section of the town. Years later, we were shocked and saddened to hear of the terrorist attack on the Westgate Shopping Mall in Westlands in 2013. The five-story mall, which opened in 2007, housing ninety stores and a multimedia cinema, was a far cry from the sleepy business area we knew and frequented in the seventies.

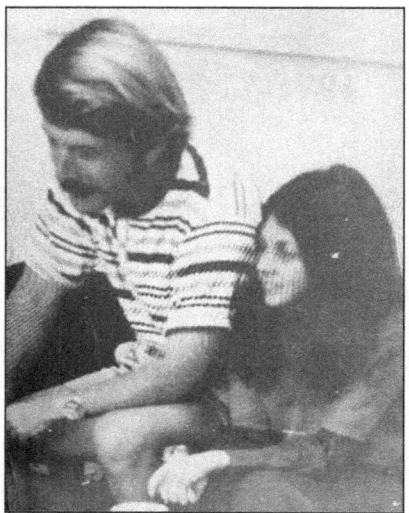

Photo of John teaching PE at NIS
John and Linda featured in the staff lounge
for the 1972 Yearbook

Nairobi International School was located on forty acres of property eight miles from the center of Nairobi in an area known as Kitusuru. The campus housed an elementary section, grades 1-6. The round elementary buildings were inspired architecturally from native huts of the indigenous people. Grades 7 through 12 were scattered in another section of the property. The school also taught college students who lived in dorms on the campus.

John coaching NIS Rugby and Basketball Teams

As with most things in life, one tends to find common ground with certain people, and they become the ones closest to you. All the teachers at NIS were great, but we bonded from the start with Norm Wiley and his adopted son, Mark. Norm was from Flint, Michigan, and taught school there before applying to the State Department for an international teaching position in Kenya. Norm had signed on with TENEA (Teacher Education in East Africa). A number of the teachers were assigned to Uganda or Tanzania, but Norm, along with his son, Mark, was sent to teach in the small town of Meru, Kenya, nestled on the northeast slopes of Mount Kenya along the Kathita River. When his contract ended, Norm applied and was offered a sixth-grade elementary teaching position at NIS and was a wealth of knowledge for all the new arrivals at the school.

Norm Wiley had rented a home in Limuru, about eighteen miles northwest of Nairobi, in an area once known as the White Highlands. Norm had horses, and he would invite us out to his beautiful home on the weekends. The girls loved to run and play on his expansive property. His son Mark was always to entertain the girls so we could visit.

Norm would often make the long drive in his Land Rover out to our little cottage in Thika to visit us on the weekends. He shared much about his life in Flint, Michigan as a teacher and how he came to adopt young Mark. We could listen to him for hours.

**Visiting Norm in the White Highlands of
Limuru Leading Tara on his horse**

I have always believed that the best storytellers are those who are willing to make themselves the self-deprecating recipient of an unfortunate experience. Norm was a master in this art form. He was a fantastic storyteller and entertained us with amusing stories of his life as a teacher in Flint. Norm would captivate us by sharing experiences in his life where he was the brunt of various catastrophic incidents that had befallen him. As he would regale us with these hilarious tales, we would be gripped in side-splitting laughter.

John had been teaching physical education from September through November when the school took a recess break for a month. December in Kenya was a lovely time of year. The short rains had ended, and the long rains wouldn't come until March.

It's hard to describe the seasons living so close to the equator. We considered December to be our summer because the weather was warm, dry, and sunny. We had been surprised to watch the lavender petals of the jacaranda trees bloom in October, a month we considered to be autumn not spring.

However, a long-time resident once explained her thoughts on Kenya's seasons to me. I had invited an elderly headmistress from Ora Drummond Kindergarten, where my girls attended school, to my home for tea. She told fascinating stories of knowing Karen Blixen and Lord Delamere in the 1920s. I wish I could remember her name. She shared, 'I believed that it is probably more accurate to say that Kenya has two springs and two autumns.' It was true that sometimes plants and trees would bloom twice in one year.

* * * * * *

One warm afternoon we were visiting with Norm Wiley at our cottage in Thika. Norm proposed that we should all go on a safari during the Christmas recess. 'Mark and I are meeting up with some other teachers to go camping in Malindi for a week. You should come.' He explained that Malindi was a lovely seaside town on the Indian Ocean just north of Mombasa.

'That sounds fun,' offered John. 'We don't have a lot of camping gear, but we have been talking about seeing more of the country and using the Volkswagen bus as a place to sleep.

I think Chris Bane's parents might loan us some camping gear. If I remove the back seat, I can take two-by-four boards, lay them across the back, and throw our mattress over it.'

'Is Malindi a town or a camping ground?' I asked Norm.

'It's a proper town just an hour north of Mombasa. It has some pleasant beach campsites right on the Indian Ocean. It's about a seven-hour drive from Nairobi. We'll drive through Tsavo National Game Park. We should see lots of elephants and other interesting game. And if you like, after we come back to Nairobi and get sorted out from camping, I thought you might like to drive into the northern desert region and visit a game park in Samburu. This time we'll stay at the lodge. There are rare species that we don't have near Nairobi like Grevy Zebra, Somali Ostrich, Reticulated Giraffe, and the long neck Gerenuk. You should see these animals.'

John and I were keen to see Kenya, so we enthusiastically said, 'Yes!'

Later that day, John confessed, 'Linda, I can't believe that I am going to have a month off from teaching. I have held down three jobs and attended college for so long. Imagine, a real holiday! I love that we made the decision to move here.'

'You have worked extremely hard. I'm happy for you, John.'

Chapter 6:
December 1971 — Safaris to
Malindi and Samburu

We were extremely excited to join Norm and other teachers on our first extended Kenya safari. We spent the next week buying or borrowing gear for our camping trip. Living in California, we grew up camping and loved spending time in the mountains. Our spirits were high as we purchased a map of Kenya and researched the areas we would be visiting. Finally, the time came to go.

A lot of the people we met remarked how beautiful and different Kenya was to their place of origin, but that was not the case with us. We felt that Kenya's climate and topography was remarkably similar to San Diego. The variety of plants we were accustomed to seeing in San Diego were replicated in Kenya. We felt right at home among the eucalyptus, bottlebrush trees, and palm trees. Bougainvillea bushes and birds of paradise plants were also familiar to us. We often marveled that San Diego had a similar climate to Kenya—the one difference being Kenya got much more rainfall.

In scientific terms, the climates were similar for these reasons. San Diego is situated on the coast of the Pacific Ocean with the desert to its east. The temperature is balmy because of the cool Alaskan current, which flows along the coast from the north. This makes for an almost perfect climate. Nairobi is situated on the equator, which should make it hot, except that the city sits on a plateau at five thousand feet in elevation, which keeps it at a pleasant temperature.

Despite my feeling very at home in Nairobi, something was not right—something was missing. It nagged me at the back of my brain, but I couldn't put my finger on what it was. I just couldn't reach out and grab it.

John outfitted the bus for camping. He removed the back seat and put our clothes and camping gear under two-by-four boards he had cut and wedged across the back of the bus. I didn't sleep well the night before we left, but the excitement of seeing more of the country energized me. We removed the full-sized mattress from our bed and placed it on top of the boards. I made up the bed with our sheets and pillows to accommodate the four of us.

One two-lane paved road stretched north and south from Nairobi to Mombasa and was the only artery for cars, tourist buses, and lorries bringing people and goods to and from the coast. In 1971 there was nothing but an open savanna on either side of the road. Baobab and thorn trees, herds of elephant and giraffe, and other wild game dominated the landscape.

During our safaris, we saw countless unique baobab trees in varying stages of their two-thousand-year lifecycle. The branches of the tree are twisted and look like roots from the ground. The elephant has a unique relationship with the baobab, which has a water-rich inner soft wood to quench their thirst on long migrations. They also eat its fruit and spread its seeds. This photo illustrates a beautiful specimen taken by my father, Bruce, on a camping trip with us just after the long rains quenched the earth in the Masai Mara region of Kenya.

Local legend says the baobab tree was too proud, so the gods uprooted them and thrust them back into the ground with their roots upside-down.

It took us three hours to arrive at an area called Voi. The tiny hamlet consisted of the one and only gas station along the entire route to Mombasa. It was where *everyone* filled up with petrol and lined up to use the rustic restroom facilities. The petrol station had a small duka—a shop—where one could purchase a variety of items at inflated prices.

As we dropped down in elevation off the high plateau of Nairobi, the weather grew warm. Our bus did not have air conditioning, so we drove with the windows down. We saw masses of wild game alongside the road cutting through Tsavo

National Game Reserve. We marveled to see herds of Masai giraffes place their long purple tongues between the thorns to graze on the tender leaves of the thorn tree. The most impressive sight was seeing vast groups of elephants walking with their young or feeding off the unusual looking Baobab trees. We must have seen them in the thousands. Over the years, I have read about the dwindling number of elephants along this road due to the constant poaching of elephants for their valuable tusks.

The heat of the day and the monotony of the road finally made me drowsy. I mentioned to John that I might want to crawl back in the rear of the bus and take a nap. Our one-year-old daughter, Tara, had just dozed off and was asleep on the mattress. Shauna expressed her delight to ride up front with her dad. The stifling heat and humidity washed over me, and I fell into a deep sleep almost immediately.

I awoke to the sound of John's voice encouraging me to sit up. 'Linda, wake up. You have to see this.' As I shook my head to clear the drowsiness, I noticed the stifling heat had slightly abated and a warm fragrant breeze was passing through the windows of the bus.

I opened my eyes and felt something had shifted. The smell overpowered me. I stretched my arms out wide and smiled. I immediately recognized the missing link that had plagued me for the last three months. It assaulted my nostrils like a briny perfume even before I even sat up. The salted air of the sea washed over me, and I breathed it in like the familiar perfume of an old friend. It finally felt like home.

* * * * * *

I was raised in an area of San Diego called North Park, which is just east of the world-famous San Diego Zoo. As the crow flies, our house on Commonwealth could not have been more than eight miles from San Diego Bay. Though to actually see the bay, I would have to climb and stand on the roof of our house, which I had done on several occasions growing up.

My friends and I considered ourselves close and intimate neighbors with the grand Pacific Ocean. We didn't have to see it to know it was there. We felt it in our souls. The Pacific Ocean was our playground. My high school boyfriend, Russell, was a surfer and our gang of friends spent our summers at South Mission Beach. The guys would take the surfboards out and catch waves. When they came to shore, the girls grabbed the boards and took turns learning to navigate the surf with the boards. We spent endless days each summer at the beach swimming, surfing, and sunbathing until our bodies turned bronze.

Often, a group of us might go to the beach at night to watch grunion wash onto the shores of Coronado or Solana Beach to spawn during high tides—knowing the phenomenon happens only in Southern California. We gathered with friends and family for evening bonfires, roasting hotdogs, and playing flag football in the sand. My dad owned a small motorboat, and he loved to take us fishing in Mission Bay. My brothers, Joe and Rob, might poach lobster or abalone hidden in the rocks off the jetty late at night for a free and easy meal.

In my entire life I had never lived further than eight miles from the sea.

* * * * * *

Recognizing the nagging piece of the puzzle that had been missing, the smell of the ocean greeted me like an old friend. I smiled.

The humid air felt fresher as I stirred on the mattress. I sat up and looked out. A strong eastern breeze blowing in from the Indian Ocean spilled through the open windows. Palm fronds swayed in the wind like the manes of wild stallions. I turned toward the ocean and saw a beautiful bare-chested young woman walking near the road balancing a load of bananas on her head. I turned away from the ocean and saw mango, papaya, and cashew nut trees in groves to the western side of the road.

As we grew closer to the city of Mombasa, the stifling heat of the savanna was becoming less intense, but the city was still warm. As we passed through the town, we saw vendors selling various wares in small carts or young men delivering goods on donkeys. The smell of roasting fish and pineapple being grilled on large steel drums made me hungry. I saw women walking in pairs along the streets of the city covered in long black robes, with only their eyes showing from inside their veils. It was my first time seeing Muslim women dressed in this manner. I wondered if the long black garments made them hot.

The ancient coastal city of Mombasa off the Indian Ocean was founded in 900 A.D and eventually became an important trade center for spices, gold, and ivory, reaching as far as India and China. Its deep bay made it the perfect port town. Throughout its history, Mombasa had been ruled by Arabs, Portuguese, and British. Toward the end of the 16th century, Fort Jesus, a World Heritage Site, was built by the Portuguese as the first successful attempt to rule the Indian Ocean trade routes from Eastern influence.

The main part of the town is centered around Mombasa Island but extends out to the mainland. The tropical climate is warm throughout the year, with its rainiest months coming between April and July.

Eventually, we headed north on a road that remained fairly close to the Indian Ocean. The countryside was more rural, but still alive with people walking alongside the road going about their business. We reached the town of Malindi and set up our camp near Norm, his son Mark, and other teachers who had come to enjoy the coastal waters of the Indian Ocean. Sandy beaches studded with palm and other types of trees led to the warm ocean with lazy waves slapping the shore. We had been told to take quinine pills to ward off malaria, which is caused by a parasite transmitted by mosquitos in tropical regions. We followed this practice for a while but gave it up after a time. We became worried about the side effects of the pills. It was a gamble, but fortunately we never contracted the disease.

Norm had brought a couple of large tire inner tubes. The next day he offered to watch the girls so we might float on the tubes in the ocean. We paddled out about twenty yards from shore and watched our girls playing in the sand, with Norm and Mark sitting nearby. We sat floating in the calm waters relaxing to the gentle swaying of swells.

All of a sudden, John started chuckling. The laughter soon grew so loud tears formed in his eyes. I couldn't imagine what might have caused this explosion of joy. I looked over where he floated next to me.

I asked him, 'John, what's so funny?'

When he finally got ahold of himself, he looked at me and said, 'Linda, I have been going to school and holding down three jobs for years. We both were working hard. I didn't think about how hard it was at the time. I just did it. Then we got this job in Kenya. Three months ago, I began teaching at NIS. Then I was told I would have a month off, with pay. I was excited that I would get to relax and finally enjoy my family.

'But all of a sudden it just hit me. Being here with you seems surreal. I mean a year ago, I would have never dreamed I would be floating with my wife on an inner tube in the Indian Ocean, watching my girls play happily in the sand.' He started laughing again. It was infectious and I joined him.

I knew John had been working hard, but raising our two small girls, I don't think I fully understood the pressure he had been under. I was extremely happy for him. Happy to be a part of his adventure and share in his joy.

'John, remember when you were doing your student teaching and taught that geography class? You came home all excited one day telling me you had taught a unit on East Africa?'

'I remember it vividly. I told you that I thought Africa would be a unique place to visit.'

'You did, and I smiled and mumbled how that would be nice, but inside I was thinking that, as the mother of two young girls, you were out of your mind. I actually cringed at the idea. Now however, I believe it might have been a strange force of nature…a foreshadowing that, in truth, we were supposed to end up here all along. It's good to see you relaxed and happy.'

At some point on our camping trip, a terrible accident happened to our friend, Norm, which we didn't fully understand until we were on the second leg of our safari in the northern desert region of Samburu. We had been camping in Malindi for five days. On occasion, we had all been washing clothes, and drying them in the sun. Norm strung his clothesline between two trees and hung his shirts, shorts, and boxer underwear to dry in the shade. We later learned from the doctor that this may have aided in his unfortunate mishap. All this was happening to Norm, but neither he nor we knew it. We packed up after our week camping.

A parasitic species called the Mango Fly is native to tropical areas of Africa like Mombasa and Malindi. Mango flies are very tiny—almost invisible to the naked eye. They lay their eggs on clothing and other material that have been air-dried outside. The larvae can survive on a host material for up to two weeks. Once they come in contact with a

mammal, they will painlessly burrow under the skin and grow. As they mature into adult maggots, it is possible to feel and see the larvae wiggling under the skin. Once the larvae fully mature, they erupt out of the skin and eventually evolve into Mango flies.

We got back to Nairobi and spent two days cleaning our camping gear and washing clothes. We planned to join Norm and Mark and drive to the northern district of Kenya and stay at a game lodge. The Samburu National Reserve is situated at the southeastern corner in the Rift Valley Province of Kenya. The area is 214 miles from Nairobi, but our old green Volkswagen bus was behaving well at this time. We arrived in Samburu in the afternoon, booked ourselves into our rooms at the lodge and met for dinner. I could see that Norm was not looking well. He seemed quiet and out of sorts. I thought he was only tired. The next day, we arranged to hire a game warden to take us into the reserve in his Land Rover to view the animals unique to the area. I was surprised when John told me that Norm would not be joining us as he didn't feel well, but Mark would be coming.

We enjoyed touring the game park and were excited to see the rare species known as Grevey zebra, giraffes, elephants, and the unusual long-neck gerenuk gazelle. Our guide pointed out a variety of beautiful bird species that sometimes get overshadowed by the bigger game, but nevertheless are spectacular. Our tour of the game park was slightly overshadowed by Norm's absence, and I hoped that nothing was seriously wrong with him.

Living in Kenya, we all had been exposed to new viruses and had been occasionally sick, so I didn't worry too much about it. I was happy that he was resting comfortably in his room. He did not join us for dinner.

The following morning John said, 'We're going to pack up and head to a small town where Norm can get treatment from a doctor.'

'Is it serious? What do you think is wrong with him?'

'Norm won't share all that much, but Mark says he's in an uncomfortable amount of pain.'

We later learned that of all the places the Mango Fly could have landed, they chose to go for Norm's boxer underwear. The larvae had embedded themselves in the area of his genitals. Mark shared that while Norm was taking a hot bath to relieve the irritation, he saw a maggot wiggle out of his skin and float to the surface of the bath water. He screamed and called his son Mark who verified Norm's worst nightmare.

John briefly shared an outline of the events, and we raced off to the nearest town where a very kind and understanding East Indian doctor extricated the remaining larvae from Norm's genital area. I didn't learn the extent of the entire problem until weeks later in Nairobi. True to Norm's self-deprecating skill as a storyteller, when he finally did share, it was hilarious.

Even now, as I recall his vivid telling of the story, I cringe. At the time, I was incredibly grateful we had dried our camping clothes in the hot equatorial sun.

Chapter 7:
1972 Kenya Harlequin Rugby Club

We were still living in the little stone cottage in Thika. John continued to enjoy his students and was making connections with other coaches from different schools to schedule games for basketball, soccer, and rugby. John felt comfortable coaching basketball and had a general knowledge of coaching soccer, but he knew nothing about rugby. He went to a coaches' meeting to schedule rugby games and sat near a fellow named John Eaton who taught at one of the English schools in the area. They struck up a conversation and John enjoyed chatting with him.

John eventually asked, 'What's the best way for me to learn how to coach a rugby team?'

Eaton replied, 'Did you ever play gridiron, Yank?'

John smiled at the gridiron reference and replied 'Yes, I played football in high school.'

'Were you any good?'

'I was a halfback, so I ran with the ball a lot. Our team won CIF championships my senior year in both football and baseball.'

Eaton looked at John and nodded his approval. 'Sounds like you already know your way around a football. Well, the best way for you to learn the game of rugby is to join one of the rugby clubs in town and play. Playing rugby will make you a better coach. I belong to Harlequins. I think you might enjoy playing for us.'

John gave Eaton our phone number and within the week, he got a call from a Scottish fellow, Dougie Hamilton, who was the captain of the team that year. He invited John to meet the team at Kenya Harlequin Rugby Club for practice the following Wednesday. He said the facility was up Ngong Road. That weekend we packed the girls in the car, did a dry run to the club to scout out the facilities.

> *The Rugby Football Union was founded in 1871 in England. A meeting with twenty-one clubs, including Harlequin F.C., was attended to establish the rules of the game and to draft a code of conduct for its members. Fifteen players would square off against the opposing side for two 40-minute continuous halves. A player must touch the rugby ball to the ground in the end zone to score a try worth five points. Two extra points can be awarded with a kicked conversion through the goal posts. A team may be awarded three points for completing a kick through the goal post when the opposition team commits a penalty. Players must lateral the ball backwards or sideways with no blocking allowed. The team with the most points wins the match.*

Wednesday came. Living in the country with no car could get boring, so John invited the girls and me to attend the five o'clock practice. There were no other wives in attendance. The girls and I sat in the stands watching the practice unfold on the rugby pitch. The team went through a series of drills, with John taking an outside position near the sideline. At one point, the ball was thrown into the middle of a mob of two sets of eight interconnected men bent over and looking like a giant spider. The rows of players joined together linking their arms over the shoulder of the man nearest him. One man threw the rugby ball into the middle of the two sides in what I later learned was called a scrum. The objective was to kick the rugby ball out the back end of the scrum, where a player, called the scrum half, stood ready to pick up the ball and lateral it backward to another player while avoiding being tackled by the opposing team. Just before being tackled to the ground, the offensive player would lateral the ball sideways to another player, all the while trying to make forward progress toward the end zone. In some ways it resembled the objectives of American football, but without shoulder pads and helmets.

It seemed like a scrappy game with little protection for the body. I saw John positioned on the outer wing and when the ball was lateraled to him, he ran forward as far as he could until he was tackled. He quickly learned that, once down, he must release the ball to avoid being penalized.

After practice, we drove home. 'What do you think, John? Are you feeling this is a sport you could coach?'

'Well, I think playing the game will help me coach the sport. In fact, they're having a game on Saturday and invited me to play. They're putting me out on the wing, which is an easier position since I don't really understand the finer points of the scrum.'

'I'm surprised they asked you to play so soon. How do you feel about that?'

'If they lateral the ball to me, I'll run until I'm tackled...just like American football. The only thing I must remember is that there are no forward passes. How hard can it be? I have to admit, I really enjoy getting to play amateur team sports again. The guys seem pretty nice.'

'I always thought it a bit unfair in America, that professional sport's players, were not allowed to play on any amateur team sports, even tennis or golf, which have nothing to do with baseball.'

'I know. Today I had so much fun, and I think I'm going to enjoy the guys and the game.'

We arrived at the rugby club on a warm Saturday morning with the girls in tow. I found an empty seat near the rest of the wives and spectators in the stands rooting for the Harlequin lads. Lots of children played with each other near the stands, and soon Shauna and Tara joined in the fun. The game was a warmup match before the regular season, which would start in a couple of weeks. I was told that our team was to play a group of young Red Berets from England who were on training exercises in the Aberdare Mountains.

Soon the game was on. I caught sight of John walking onto the pitch in his new white shorts and black knee-high socks to take his position on the right wing. He had yet to purchase football cleats, so he just played in his trainers. Someone had given him a Harlequin jersey. He looked like he belonged.

Although John knew nothing about rugby, in high school he was an all-city fullback for his Crawford High School football team. In fact, both his baseball and football teams had won CIF championships in 1962. He was also chosen on the all-star roster, *Breitbard Athletic Foundation,* for all-city schools in both sports. Even though John was not familiar with the fundamentals of rugby, as a halfback he knew how to run with a football in his hands.

At some point in the game, his teammates from Quins lateraled the rugby ball out to John, who was closest to the sidelines in the wing position. John tucked the ball in his arms and started running. Several members of the Red Berets tried to tackle him but without success. He stormed past the opposing team and charged into the end zone. Unlike American football, he was unaware that he needed to touch the ball on the ground to score the try (goal). He heard screams from his teammates yelling at him to place the ball on the ground. He was able to do so just before running past the dead ball line (the end zone) which would have made the try invalid.

Harlequin captain Dougie Hamilton ran over to congratulate him. 'Not bad for your first game of rugby, Yank. Now if you get your hands on the ball again and score a try, place the ball on the grass directly under the goal posts for an easier kick.'

John nodded and the game continued. At some point, the ball was again lateraled to his position on the wing, and with the ball tucked under his arm, he charged in for his second goal, this time placing it directly under the goalpost. An article from the *East African Standard* told the story but neglected to mention the American's first name in the article.

Red Berets Miss a Good Kicker
East African Standard Staff Reporter

The score at Ngong Road yesterday was 23-22. The teams were Kenya Harlequins v. 1ˢᵗ Logistics Regiment, 16 Ind. Para. Brigade. Quins won but only just — and it looked as if the injury hoodoo had struck again because Harrison was taken off early with a suspected dislocated shoulder.

This was a case of Quins being too long in the tooth and the Paras being too long in the Aberdares. Given a kicker, Pares would have won the game. Given fitness, Quins would have walked all over these blokes in the Red Berets.

The man of the match was Allison of Quins. OK? So, they had to tell him to touch the ball down just before the dead ball line, but he scored twice by running — and that is how you do it in East Africa.

During the following Wednesday's practice, John walked into the clubhouse. A player named Tony Glover was sitting at the bar reading the newspaper. Without looking up, and seemingly talking to no one in particular, he said in a loud voice, 'It was the oddest thing. I was down at the New Stanley Hotel trying to buy a newspaper last Sunday, but the clerk said this American bloke had been in earlier that morning and bought up every copy of the Standard.' He shot a glance over at John and gave him a mischievous grin.

John laughed and knew he had found just the home he had been looking for.

* * * * * *

Harlequin Scrum, John standing at the back.
Rugby Lineout, John at the far end of the line.

There were many rugby clubs in Kenya in 1972. The country had only gained its independence in December of 1963. Although many colonials chose to leave Kenya and go to Great Britian or other Commonwealth countries, some of the expatriates chose to stay, and they carried on with many of the traditions they had enjoyed as colonialists. Most of the clubs' players consisted of these white expatriates and colonial settlers. The towns of Thika, Kitale, Naivasha, and Mombasa maintained clubs outside the city, while the Nondies, Impala, and Harlequin clubs resided in Nairobi. The newly formed republic was in transition to eventually blend colonial traditions into the new ideals of an emerging republic.

The effect of WWI and WWII accelerated the gradual breakup of the British Empire. As more countries vied for their independence, the United Kingdom offered a free association of sovereign states that would be known as the Commonwealth of Nations. Those members of its former dependencies who joined, would maintain ties of friendship and practical cooperation with Great Britian, and acknowledge the British monarch as the symbolic head of their association. Australia, New Zealand, and Canada became the first to join in 1931. At the time of its independence in 1963, Kenya also chose to join the British Commonwealth. The objectives of the Commonwealth and its member states began with the ideals to express a commitment to the development of a free and democratic society and the promotion of peace and prosperity to improve the lives of its members. Today, two billion people from fifty-two independent countries from all over the world, with various cultures, languages, and races, make up its membership.

When we joined Harlequins in early 1972, we were the only Americans in the club. The members were welcoming, and we were beginning to make new friends. What we didn't understand, as new members, were certain protocols between the husbands and their wives. One protocol had been a standard practice for years and involved teams traveling for away games.

John was quickly learning the game of rugby and enjoyed the team aspect of the club. He soon became friendly with teammate John Maynard, a scrappy prop forward. John liked Maynard's zest for life and was captivated by his easy-going personality and gift for singing rugby songs. Maynard introduced us to his wife, Audrey, and they became the first friends we connected with at the club. The Maynards hailed from Yorkshire and soon had us over for dinner, where we enjoyed an authentic *Roast Beef and Yorkshire Pudding* meal. Their daughters, Heather and Louise, were similar in age to our girls. We were delighted to get to know them better, but as with so many expatriates in Kenya, John and Audrey left Kenya several months after we joined the club to return to England. We were sad to see them go.

Later, after we had put the girls down for the night, John relayed his conversation with John Maynard with me after a practice in early March.

> *Maynard announced to John, 'Hey Allison, the team is playing an away game in Kitale this weekend. Think you might be able to come?'*
>
> *'Where's that?'*
>
> *'It's on the other side of the Rift Valley in the highlands near Eldoret. Some of the English colonialists chose to stay in Kenya after its independence and continue to farm and raise livestock in the region. The farmers are tough blokes and play a mean game of rugby.'*
>
> *'Sure. Can I bring Linda and the girls?'*
>
> *After a few moments, the easy-going Maynard shrugged his shoulders and said, 'I guess—I think that would be okay.'*

'I thought you and the girls would like to see more of Kenya.'

'Would other families go?'

'I'm not sure, but Maynard thought it would be okay to bring you and the girls.'

'Where would we stay?'

'After the match, the Kitale side will host us for dinner and dancing, and we'll all be parceled out to stay at one of the various farms for the night. We'll drive out early Saturday and come back to Nairobi Sunday afternoon.'

I was pleased that John was enjoying rugby and happy that he wanted to include us in the experience. I responded, 'It'll be fun to see more of the country.'

We drove out of Nairobi early to meet the team in Kitale the following Saturday. The long rains had just begun, and the floor of the Rift Valley was turning green with new grass. Several herds of impala and Cape Buffalo grazed on the valley floor. We climbed up the western side of the escarpment and arrived at the Kitale club early that afternoon. I was surprised to see no other Harlequin wives in attendance but didn't think too much about it. The Kitale wives were extremely hospitable, hosting us to a wonderful buffet dinner. After an evening of dancing, we were invited to one of the players' farms for the night. The farmhouse was a sprawling one-story ranch style that I could tell had expanded over the years with various wings. On Sunday, we were treated to a huge breakfast and a tour of the farm before heading back to Nairobi.

The following Wednesday, John came home from practice and said, 'Well, I guess we ruffled a few feathers among the wives, Linda!'

'What do you mean?'

'Some of the guys said they got quite an earful when the wives heard that the American player had brought his wife to an away game.'

I could see where this was heading, and it became clear to me why I had seen no other Harlequin wives in Kitale. 'What happened?'

'I guess it's *standard practice* that wives DO NOT come on away games.'

'Oh dear.'

'I didn't know,' John said throwing his hands up.

Nothing more was said about the 'American wife' who broke protocol, but for the rest of our years with the club, *all* the wives and families traveled with the men to away games.

The Brits are great storytellers, they love to laugh, and delight in sharing self-deprecating stories whenever they get the chance. And we loved them for it. However, being Americans, we didn't understand all the nuances of the British culture, which is steeped in thousands of years of tradition. We slowly learned these traditions over time.

There is a protocol for just about everything! For example—When you finish a meal, the knife and fork must be placed together on your plate at six and twelve o'clock to let the server know you are done eating—One must never put jam on your toast during the savory egg course, jam on toast comes later—When eating, the fork stays in the left hand and the knife in the right. Americans are continuously admonished for our inefficient use of the knife and fork—Tea is drunk first thing in the morning because it's more refreshing than coffee and again, all throughout the day...well just because Brits love tea—When traveling, it doesn't matter where you are but it is imperative to stop for coffee and cake mid-morning—Pudding is a name for dessert, but dessert isn't always a pudding—All holidays are known simply as *bank holidays* except for Guy Fox Day on November 5th, which is a holiday to commemorate a man who tried to blow up Parliament.

Rugby is a unique team sport, and it was foreign to John's experience playing team sports in America. After a rugby match, John delighted in witnessing the host and visiting teams gather in the bar area of the club to drink beer and sing dirty rugby songs for hours. No matter how rough and contentious it got on the pitch, the players were happy to drink a Shandy (a mix of beer and sparkling lemon soda) or a beer and belt out a litany of clever rugby songs. It was a new experience for John, and he loved the camaraderie of singing after a game.

Each member of Harlequins had a special song that he sang at some point during the evening. Everyone knew that particular song was his. John Maynard held ownership of a jazzy little number called, *Dan, Dan, the Lavatory Man.* Dougie Hamilton led the lads in a song about a girl named *Peggy O'Neal* who rides a bike with one wheel. Bob Shepard directed the boys in *The Lobster Song,* about a man who buys a lobster late at night, takes it home to his wife and puts it in the toilet. You can only imagine what disaster ensues.

The team was preparing to go to Mombasa for an away game. Captain Dougie Hamilton took John aside and said, 'John, you're going to need to produce a song for the trip. It will become your song.'

John came home in a state of panic. He loved the guys'
songs but couldn't think of a clever, slightly naughty song that
might amuse his teammates.

'You have to help me, Linda. You're always singing.'

'Gee, I don't know, John.'

'You must know something that'll work.'

We racked our brains for an hour until finally a tune
emerged from my childhood.

'The only song I can think of that might work is one my
dad used to amuse us with in the car when we were little kids.'

'I'm getting desperate. What is it?'

'You won't believe it, but it's an old Bing Crosby song
from the thirties. I think. It's funny and a little naughty. It's
called *Huggin' and A Chalkin.'*

'Can you sing it for me?'

'I'm not sure the words are exactly right, but Dad sang it
like this:

Oh Gee, but ain't it great to have a girl so big and fat,
that when you go to hug her, you don't know where you're at.
You have to take a piece of chalk in your hand,
and hug away and chalk away to see where you began.
One day, I was a huggin' and a chalkin' and a beggin' her to
be my bride,
when I met another fella with some chalk in his hands,
Comin' around the other side.
Over the mountain. O'er the great divide.'

John laughed and said he thought the song would be enough to secure his place at the team sing-along. He shared the story with me when he got home. 'Fortified with a few pints of beer, I belted it out for the guys in Mombasa, and it was well-received.'

So, for the next year, John took ownership of the Bing Crosby song, *Huggin' and a Chalkin',* which he performed after the games. Today, the song would be considered completely inappropriate, but I guess it was acceptable in the thirties.

Life could be quite fluid in Kenya. Players and families were coming and going all the time. We were sad when teammate Tony Glover and his wife Gill left for a new job in the Seychelles shortly after we joined the club. John had formed an attachment with Tony after the write-up after John's first game in the newspaper, and Tony's teasing him about it.

One day he came home from practice excited. 'Guess what? Bob Shepherd is leaving Kenya, and he gifted me his song! You know the one about the Lobster man. I always loved that song, and he gave it to ME.' So, the Bing Crosby song was retired, and *The Lobster Song* was officially willed to John.

I cautioned, 'That's great, John. That one is *very* funny and *very* naughty. Promise me you won't sing it around the girls.' Of course, he did. In fact, we soon began to sing all the dirty rugby songs while driving in the car. We got very clever about changing the words to clean them up for our kids' ears.

Years later on a trip to England in the nineties, John and I visited Dougie Hamilton and his wife Margaret, who had left Kenya and lived in Sherborne, England.

I asked Dougie, who was still very much involved in rugby, 'Do the players in England gather after the rugby games and sing the songs like in Kenya?'

Dougie sadly shook his head in the negative. 'When the new drinking laws came into effect in England, it put an end to the after-match sing-alongs. Too many players feared getting pulled over by the police and getting a ticket for drinking. Today, the players go home as soon as the game is over. In fact, the rugby songs are slowly fading into oblivion. It's sad. I believe the younger rugby players will not know the songs in a decade.' It made us a little melancholy because it really was a wonderful tradition.

* * * * * *

Harlequins was not only a place to play rugby, but it became the center of our social lives. We had only been members of the club for a few weeks, when it was announced that the club would hold a western-themed dance, and we should all dress in costume. I put something together, found a feather and braided my hair to look like an Indian girl. John owned a serape and came as a Clint Eastwood-inspired cowboy. We were told that some of the men would entertain us with cowboy songs and skits. We were bemused to watch the Brits, in cowboy hats and Indian feathers, huddle around a fake campfire singing western songs.

After several of these themed dances, it occurred to me that only the men were invited to be a part of these entertainment cabarets. By this time, I had made friends with two of the members' wives, Jan Ellis and Sue Evans. Jan's husband, John, played on the team and Sue's husband, Rob, was a non-playing member. The girls were great fun, and we were developing close ties.

I invited them to my house for an afternoon of coffee and cake. After the initial conversation, I asked, 'Why is it that only the men participated in the entertainment at the dances? Jan, you have a lovely voice. I've heard you sing at the Hootenanny in Hurlingham.'

Jan shrugged her shoulders and said, 'I'm not sure.'

Jan Bradley Ellis was a Kenya girl and the third child of an English colonial expatriate who married a lovely East Indian woman. Jan sang with her brother and sister in and around Nairobi and were known as the Bradley Trio. She was a beautiful girl, and her looks mirrored her lovely personality. Jan had married a Harlequin teammate, John Ellis from Yorkshire, just before we had arrived.

'Jan, I've 'heard you sing at functions in Nairobi and on the radio with your siblings. You have a beautiful voice. Sue, you also have a lovely soprano voice. I have an idea.'

'Oh no. Here she goes,' teased Sue. 'What bossy American scheme do you have in mind for us today.'

'Well, funny you should ask. You know how the guys like to entertain with songs and skits at the dances.'

'Yes. What's in that mind of yours, Linda?' asked Sue.

'Well, I was thinking. The next dance at the club is going to be a circus theme, you know, with everyone coming in costume.'

'Right,' they chorused.

'Well, I play the guitar and thought maybe the three of us could put something together and sing a few songs.' The girls were silent for a few moments. I assumed they were quietly contemplating my suggestion.

'I don't know, Linda. I think it would be fun, but it's never been done before,' offered Jan.

'Why not? Personally, I think we might do better than some of stuff I've heard the men put out. What about you, Sue?'

'I don't think it would hurt to give it a go. If we don't like how we sound, no one will ever need to know we tried,' said Sue.

I knew the chords and harmony to Simon and Garfunkel's *Feeling Groovy*. (Remember it was the early seventies!) We decided to start with that. During our next secret rehearsal, I shared a tape of Astrud Gilberto's song about a *Circus Parade*. We agreed that it would be a good choice to go with the circus-themed party. We learned that fast-paced number and decided we sounded good enough to ask if we could be a part of the cabaret. We proposed the idea to a few of the members and they reluctantly said it would *probably* be okay to add a few more songs to their established program.

The big night arrived. Jan was accustomed to singing in public and we allowed her strong voice to carry us along. Sitting on stools, we performed our two songs at the circus-themed dance. Our numbers were met with praise from *most* of the members. There were a few of the men from the old guard who were not pleased that we had butted in. But from that time forward, women were slowly allowed to join in on the entertainment.

Over time, the male members came to accept the women as regular participants at the cabaret performances at all the dances. In 1974 many countries were celebrating *The Year of the Woman.* The wives collaborated with some of the male members to produce a show. We delighted the audience with skits and songs to highlight and spoof the accomplishments of women throughout the years and into the future.

Sue, Linda, and Jan Singing at Harlequins—1974

Chapter 8:
1972 – Benedictine and the CIA

After our camping experience with Chris Bane in the Aberdares, a relationship with his parents bloomed during our first months in Kenya. We had been invited to Howard and Anita Bane's home many times for dinner. They were very generous and would at times gift us with a bottle of vodka, scotch, or a fancy liqueur, like Benedictine. The bottles were stamped *Property of the American Embassy*, and the prices were always marked $2.00. Even in the seventies, this was an amazing deal for the employees working at the embassy. We kept the liquor on hand for guests. Howard and Anita were Catholic and had a large family. They knew that we also were Catholic and did not make a big salary at NIS. It was clear that they wanted to make our lives in Kenya a little easier.

At about this same time, we were having trouble with our ayah, Rose. We suspected that she had been nipping into the liquor bottles gifted to us courtesy of Howard and the embassy. One evening, John noticed that the bottles from our liquor supply seemed to be evaporating and asked my thoughts on the matter.

'If this is true, it's not good, John. Should we confront Rose about this?'

'Let's sit on it for a day or two. Bottom line, we can't have her stealing from us, Linda. If she's drinking, she may not be as watchful with Shauna and Tara on the days you are called in to teach. Plus, she may be stealing other things from us.'

'What are we going to do?'

'I'll mark the bottles and see if the level drops.'

That night, after releasing Rose to her quarters, we got to work placing small inconspicuous marks on each of our bottles. The next night, we checked the marks, and as we suspected, some of the bottles had receded a half inch. It appeared that Rose had a special affinity for our bottle of Benedictine liqueur.

The next day we approached her on the subject and her demeanor confirmed our suspicions. We gave her notice that our time together had come to an end. We settled her wages and suggested she go home to her village. John said he would drive her to the bus depot the following morning on his way to school. Unfortunately, when the next morning came, Rose refused to leave. She barricaded herself in her servant's quarters and would not come out.

I felt sorry for her. Rose was lonely, young, and probably felt she had failed her family. But we had to let her go. John drove our bus over to Mr. Guthega's house and explained the issue. We hoped he wouldn't be upset with us as he was the one who had suggested her.

Our landlord said, 'Do not worry about this, bwana, I will take care of the problem.'

Later that morning, I was shocked when two policemen showed up at our door and carted young Rose off to jail in a police car. I was frantic and called NIS. John said he would stop by Mr. Guthega's house on his way home from school.

Late that afternoon, John showed up at our house with a very remorseful Rose. She sheepishly made her way to her servant's quarters and closed the door.

'What happened, John?'

'I stopped by Mr. Guthega's house and told him we did not want Rose to be prosecuted or sent to jail. We just wanted her gone. He called the police station and told them I would be coming to get her, and they should release her to me. Naturally, Rose was a bit shaken when she saw me. We talked on the way here, and she promised she would pack her things and leave tomorrow morning. I agreed to drive her to the bus station.'

* * * * * *

In April, we got two weeks off for the Easter break, and Howard and Anita invited us to join their family at a beautiful duplex courtesy of the American Embassy. We later learned it was property retained for the specific uses of the CIA. The duplex was situated just north of the main city of Mombasa. The Bane's family occupied one side of the duplex, and we were given the adjoining two-bedroom unit for our family. The duplex and gardens were built on a cliff overlooking the turquoise waters of the Indian Ocean. A winding path led down the slope past a stone retaining wall to the beautiful white sandy beach and ocean. A week of swimming, fishing, and sunbathing was a dream come true for us. We couldn't believe how kind and thoughtful a gesture it was. Unbeknown to us, during this time, Howard was studying and gaining intel on us.

The only downside to our week was not realizing how intense the equatorial sun could be. Despite putting suntan lotion on, we all got a bit sunburnt. Tara was hit the hardest. I felt terrible for her. It was a lesson learned. Or so I thought. The trip to Mombasa was just the tonic we needed, and we both felt refreshed and ready to tackle the rest of our first year at NIS.

View of Indian Ocean with the girls from CIA Duplex

**Mombasa photos taken at the Bane family CIA Duplex—
1972**

* * * * * *

Sometime in early 1972, young Chris Bane began playing rugby for Harlequins. Howard took an immense interest in coming to the games and weekly practices. While Howard was learning to enjoy the game of rugby, we eventually learned that we were being gradually assessed for undercover work for the CIA. Howard later told us it was an opportunity to interact and connect with John and me as potential undercover assets. Howard was a veteran agent for the CIA. He and Anita, along with their children had been assigned to various countries throughout the world, and Howard climbed steadily up the ranks of the CIA. In Kenya, Howard held the top job of Chief of Station.

Among his many achievements, Howard Bane acted as the ground Case Officer in India in charge of the exfiltration of the Dalai Lami from Tibet. Howard served his country well and was called out of retirement to assist in special operations after 911.

Howard Bane (left) with the Dalai Lami, and Ambassador Bunker — Extraction from Tibet

An excerpt from an article written about Howard Bane's service to the CIA in **The Washington Times,** *by John B. Roberts August 2, 2007, shortly after Bane's passing, says it best.*

Howard's 39-year career exemplifies the best of the CIA. He held the distinguished Intelligence Medal, the CIA's highest award, and spent more than 20 years in overseas posts. Early in this career, Howard showed an astonishing ability to pitch and recruit agents. After September 11, Howard and other "reemployed annuitants" kept vital functions going so that the agency could rapidly staff up overseas stations with experienced younger officers. Men and women, like Howard, who continued their service in their golden years, did it because it was the right and honorable thing to do.

John called from school in April saying Howard wanted him to stop by his house on the way home. When he arrived home later that night, he sat me down and told me that Howard wanted us to come and work for the CIA. I was stunned.

'But you have a job at NIS. It sounds like it might be dangerous.'

'Just hear me out. It would be a terrific opportunity for us, Linda. I know how lonely you have been here in the country.

Howard wants to move us into a two-story duplex in Hurlingham. There is a Middle Eastern family occupying the ground floor apartment and we would move into the upper apartment. It would be a step up for us. We would be living in the city with a much easier drive to school. The suburb of Hurlingham is just off Ngong Road and close to Harlequins. Oh, and President Kenyatta's State house is about two blocks away from the property. It's a really nice neighborhood.'

I was taken aback but promised I would be willing to hear what Howard was offering. John said, 'It will take several weeks to be vetted. I will have to take a polygraph test, and they might interview some of our neighbors in San Diego.'

'Really?'

'It's standard stuff. The agency wants to assess our characters. Howard said they might ask if we are known to be upstanding US citizens, or if we have ever been part of any organization working against national security.'

'Well, that should be easy. I think our neighbors will say cordial things about us. Why do they want us to work for them? They must have their own people doing this type of work.'

'I'm sure they do, but Howard said that we are in Kenya under contract with Nairobi International School. In other words, we have a legitimate reason for being in the country and we are not connected with the US government in any capacity. He thinks we would make perfect assets to do undercover work for the CIA without drawing suspicion to us.'

'Would we be compensated for our service? Lord knows we could use the money. The school is behind on our salary and housing allotment again.'

'Yes. There are lots of details to work out, but Howard said the agency would cover the rental cost of our duplex, and we would receive a monthly operations stipend in Kenyan shillings. Because we also get a housing allotment from the school, Howard said the agency's payments would be deposited directly in our bank account in San Diego and could not be traced to the CIA. Howard suggested that we not access that account while in Kenya, but it would be waiting for us when we return home to the states.'

I was a little dazed by John's news but excited with the thought of moving out of the country and into town. 'It's a lot to take in, but I can see it's a wonderful opportunity for us.'

'I think Howard really cares about us and wants us to live in a safer environment. He mentioned his concern for us living in the country so far from Nairobi. Let's sleep on it. Howard wants us to come for dinner on Friday. We should have an answer for him by then.'

During the dinner with Anita and Howard, they answered all our questions. We began gradually moving forward with the vetting process to work for the CIA. We were under strict orders from Howard to keep our relationship with the CIA secret from any friends and family in Kenya or abroad. Howard told us we should be ready to take possession of the property in Hurlingham in August.

* * * * * *

Our first school year at NIS came to an end in June, and we signed a new contract to teach for the next year. John continued to play rugby for Harlequins and the club became an ever-important part of our social life.

During June, we were busy preparing our little cottage to accommodate four adult guests for a month. Just before they were scheduled to arrive, we received another lucky break. An American family with students at NIS was moving back to the United States and offered to sell us their little Fiat as a second car. It was a welcome addition to the old green Volkswagen, which continued to give us trouble from time to time.

In July of 1972, my parents came for a visit with two women from our church in San Diego who had recently lost their husbands. Marie Ursich and Maureen Nettles were good sports about sleeping on camp cots in the living room. Although we were crammed into our tiny cottage, it was wonderful having friends and family from home stay with us. My parents spoiled the girls with a tricycle for Tara and a baby buggy for Shauna's doll.

Several days after our guests' arrival, John decided to take a day trip to Amboseli Game Park, situated at the base of Mount Kilimanjaro to show Bruce, Marie, and Maureen the annual wildebeest migration. Shauna went with the group. Mom and I stayed back with Tara and promised to cook a delicious roast beef dinner for them that evening with all the trimmings. When they hadn't returned by 9:00 PM, we grew worried, so I called our good friend, Norm Wiley. He connected with the police, and we were relieved that no crashes had been reported on the road from Amboseli to Nairobi. Norm promised to come over the next morning. There was nothing more we could do, so we retired for an uneasy night of sleep.

By mid-morning, I received a call from John saying that the bus had broken down as they were off-roading in the park, and they had to stay the night on a dried riverbed. Norm came to the rescue. He and I drove to the park in his Land Rover. We found them in the game lodge, and they took us out to the bus, which we towed back to Nairobi for repair.

That evening we heard the whole story from Shauna, who was more than a little traumatized by the whole affair.

'We first went to eat at the lodge, but the waiter said we had missed lunch. They could only feed us little sandwiches and tea. Daddy said it was okay because Mommy and Grandma were making us a big dinner at home. Then we went looking for animals. The bus wouldn't start, so we had to stay the night in the dark. It was really cold inside the bus, but daddy kept me warm in the front seat until morning. Daddy was brave and walked all the way to a road and got a ride to the lodge. Then some rangers came and took us all back to the lodge. I was *really* hungry, but the waiter said we had missed breakfast and all he could give us was little sandwiches and tea. The day before I ate slowly, so I didn't get as many little sandwiches as the others. This time, I tugged on daddy's shirt and made him promise that Grandpa and the ladies wouldn't eat all the little sandwiches again.'

'You were brave too,' I said.

Linda looking at John and Bruce in Matching Safari Outfits—1972

On his first visit, Dad wanted to purchase safari gear and talked John into doing so too. John hated looking like a tourist, but he loved my dad and went along with it. We laughed at the photos later.

We wanted to show our guests as much of Kenya as we could. Dad rented a car to take trips to Nairobi Game Park and Ngong Hills near Nairobi. In the course of our stay in Nairobi, we often spent time at Ngong Hills flying kites with the kids or on a picnic. The beautiful hills afforded a view of Nairobi Game Park to the east. From the west, a 1000-foot drop revealed Masai villages dotted along the Great Rift Valley. At one of the four peaks, we enjoyed walking to an area with an obelisk and small garden that marked the grave of an early colonial settler.

In 1980, we were delighted to see the movie *Out of Africa* with Meryl Streep and Robert Redford shot on location in Kenya. It was then we realized that the obelisk and grave was of Denys Finch-Hatton, whose character was portrayed by Redford. (The burial site in the movie *was* on Ngong Hills but not the location of the actual burial spot.)

Flying kites at Ngong Hills with the Great Rift Valley below—1976

The old bus was finally repaired and made it up to the White Highlands located in the central uplands of Kenya. The highlands had been sparsely inhabited by the indigenous people of Kenya in the early colonial days and European settlers realized the value of its agricultural productivity. Tea, coffee, sisal, and pyrethrum were profitable crops for the colonialists. By 1930, sixty-five percent of the highlands had been reserved for European settlers as an incentive came to Kenya and farm.

We were stunned at beautiful the scenery with its vast verdant fields of tea and coffee. We stopped at the Highlands Hotel for lunch and to purchase Kisii carvings made from soapstone. It was easy to envision colonial life before Kenya won its independence in this beautiful region of land.

Howard and Anita graciously treated us and our guests to another stay in Mombasa. The duplex, overlooking the Indian Ocean, was made available to us. The Banes surprised us by offering us the *entire* duplex for a week, with my parents and the two women using one side and our family occupying the other. The week's stay was a very generous offer and the highlight of our family's visit to Kenya.

We took both cars and made the six-hour journey to Mombasa. We passed through Tsavo National Game Park and our guests marveled at seeing massive herds of elephants along the roadside. One of the workers at NIS, Benjamin, agreed to join us as our houseboy to cook and clean for some extra cash. He entertained us with his stories of learning English at a missionary school. We experienced the joy of Benjamin seeing the ocean for the first time in his life. Benjamin couldn't swim but allowed my dad to take him floating on a plastic raft in the shallow waves. Benjamen would let us know, 'I am safe. Bruce is my guide.'

The embassy had an arrangement with a beautiful hotel next door allowing guests of the duplex to use the large swimming pool and other facilities. We enjoyed swimming at the hotel pool. Tara was only two but learned to swim using inflatable arm bands. John kept releasing the air until, without her knowing it, she was swimming on her own. I thought I had learned my lesson from our previous visit, but as vigilant as I was putting sun lotion on the girls, Tara ended up with another sunburned face.

One morning, while sitting on the patio drinking coffee, we observed what appeared to be a group of convicts building a house on the property next to us. Armed guards stood near while other men coordinated the work. My dad thought it would be interesting to snap a few photos. He knew to be discreet, but a watchful soldier sensed that something seemed amiss. He marched over to us and demanded that my father give him his camera. John did some fast talking and explained that his father-in-law was merely cleaning his camera. The soldier was not happy and said he would have to confiscate the 35 mm film inside the Pentax. John was always great at smoothing things over. He shared casually that we were staying at the duplex as the guests of the American Embassy. When the soldier heard this, he reluctantly allowed my father to keep his camera and his film. We later learned that the property was owned by Vice President Daniel arap Moi. It was easy to see why the government might not want photos of prison convicts being used to build his beach house.

Later that evening when we were alone, John said, 'You'll have to talk to your dad, Linda. I know he didn't mean anything, but we don't want to draw any attention to us right now.'

'I'll talk to him and remind him we are in a foreign country and to be more cautious in the future.'

The weeks flew by, and we sadly said goodbye to our family and guests in late July. The next day we gave notice to Mr. Guthega that we would be moving closer to town in August.

Bruce taking photo with convicts working on the vice president's home. The shot nearly got us in trouble with the Kenya police

Chapter 9:
August 1972 {Code Names} Betsy and Babe

The two-bedroom furnished apartment in Hurlingham was perfect for our family. The top floor of the duplex had a ground-level exterior door to the right of our home. Entering the duplex, we encountered stairs, consisting of manufactured stone. The interior stairs led halfway up to a small landing, turned left with more stairs leading directly into the parlor of our living space. There was no door, so I cautioned the girls to be incredibly careful. A fall could be extremely dangerous on such a solid stone surface. The stairs had an echo, and the girls enjoyed playing on the landing and singing.

The house consisted of an adjoining living and dining room. A small kitchen with an exterior door led to a small outdoor balcony, which we used to dry laundry. Two bedrooms and one bathroom completed the floorplan. The transfer to our new home was fairly easy, as we did not have a lot of possessions. We were thrilled to be situated in town, especially now that I had the little Fiat to run around town. My first agenda was setting up the house and hiring our new houseboy,

As often happened in Kenya, when one family leaves, they might suggest a good houseboy for those looking to hire one. That's how George Washington Ochieng came to work for us. George's Luo tribe lived near the eastern shores of Lake Victoria. We were lucky to find him, and he stayed with us for the remainder of our time in Kenya as a trusted part of our family.

* * * * * *

We were gradually being groomed for our tasks with the agency. A CIA case officer or handler named Fred was assigned to us. He invited us to his house to meet and sign confidentiality documents. Fred was about as unassuming a spy as one could imagine. He reminded me of Don Knotts, the bumbling deputy, Barney Fife, on the TV show set in the rural town of Mayberry. I'm not sure what I was expecting, but Fred certainly wasn't it. He was small in stature and looked more like an accountant or an insurance salesman than a secret agent. I later came to understand that looks could be deceiving. Fred was incredibly good at his job.

Fred met us at the door of his home, escorted us to his office and closed the door. In an effort to put us at ease, the first thing he did was to share his prized collection of Playboy Magazines.

'I'm proud to say I have collected every issue of Playboy going all the way back to the first edition.' To prove his point, Fred went to where his magazines were displayed and pulled out the 1953 Playboy Magazine featuring Marilyn Monroe on the cover. We nodded and expressed our admiration, not knowing what else to say on the subject.

'Let's get down to business. I will be your case officer. Any questions you might have, or any dealings as we go forward, will be explicitly handled through me. You will meet other agents from time to time, but you will talk to no one else at the embassy about your assignments or any problem you may encounter. The exception to that would be Howard Bane. Do you understand?'

'We understand.'

Fred pulled out a contract, which showed that we would receive a monthly allowance for our new rental property, which would be automatically deposited in our bank account in San Diego and a small monthly stipend for our services, which would be paid in Kenyan shillings. Part of our new contract with NIS included a monthly housing allowance for our new place in Hurlingham. We were delighted that the housing allowance, from the CIA would be deposited into our banking account in San Diego, which we vowed never to touch while in Kenya.

Fred showed us our contracts and told us to pick out our code names. We looked confused. 'All future communications and receipts for any money needed for various operations or to take possession of a device loaned to you by the CIA will be signed using your code names.'

We discussed one or two options, which Fred rejected.

'I suggest you keep the names simple. Pick the name of a famous person, so you won't forget it.' We discussed several options over the next few minutes.

John settled on the code name Babe, in honor of the famed baseball player Babe Ruth. I chose the name, Betsy, for the woman who is thought to have sewn the first American Flag during the American Revolutionary War, Betsy Ross. From that moment, all of our interactions with Fred and the CIA were signed using our code names Betsy and Babe.

'Have you met your neighbors yet?' asked Fred.

'We've introduced ourselves to the Middle Eastern family that lives below us and their daughter, Mona, who is a little older than our girls. Mohammed works as a diplomat for his embassy and Babekka is a housewife. They seem really nice,' I offered.

'That's great, Linda. Your job will be to become friendly with them. Get them to trust you. Have them up for drinks or tea. I would keep the conversation away from politics but find out all you can about their lives and who they see socially. Our intel tells us that Mohammed and Babekka are friendly with a suspected Russian KGB operative who lives next door to you. His name is Sergei. See if you can get an introduction there, but don't press it.'

We nodded in understanding. Fred gave us a few small jobs, which seemed easy enough. We were to visit a series of post offices each week and empty the contents, which we would pass to Fred. 'A lot of mail will be coming from various places in Uganda. We are in secret communication with our people there and what's going on with the dictator, Idi Amin. *All* the mail should be passed on to us, even if it looks unimportant. '

We concluded our meeting with an arrangement to meet Fred in town for a handoff of the post office box mail and receive further instructions.

Chapter 10:
September 1972 – Our First Operation

We liked our downstairs Middle Eastern neighbors. (In writing this memoir, I have been instructed not to name their country of origin.) Mohammed insisted that we call him Moe. He and Babekka were friendly and easy to be around. My girls played in the large grassy area in front of our duplex with their daughter, Mona. Mohammed worked for his embassy and came home for lunch each afternoon. The heavenly scent of garlic and other spices wafted up through Babekka's kitchen into my kitchen window, and I would think, *Moe is a lucky man.* I reminded myself to ask her about some of her dishes, as it seemed we both shared a love of cooking. After lunch, Mohammed liked to sit on his front porch with a glass of hot tea. I often was invited to join them in the shade of their porch.

'Moe, I notice that you aways drink your hot tea from a glass. Is this the custom in your country?'

Mohammed held up his small glass and admired the clear dark liquid. 'I have never been asked this question before, Linda. I suppose it's because I like to look at the amber color of the tea through the glass.'

'It is beautiful, Moe' I remarked.

Mohammed turned his attention from his glass and said, 'This reminds me, Babekka and I are giving a party with the various friends we have made in Nairobi and some of my work colleagues. It will be a week from Saturday. We would love it if you and John would join us. There will be a light buffet supper and drinks…very casual…not a sit-down affair.'

'That's kind of you. I'll talk to John and get back to you. What time were you thinking?'

'Any time after 8:00 PM. It's very informal.'

John and I relayed the information to our case officer, Fred. He seemed incredibly happy that the friendship was progressing. He asked us to meet him later that week for coffee at the Thorn tree Café in Nairobi.

'This cocktail party will be your first big assignment.'

'What do you want us to do?' asked John.

'It sounds as though lots of guests will be in attendance.'

I nodded. 'Mohammed said they were planning on about twenty guests for cocktails and a light buffet supper. He said it would be a casual affair.'

'That's perfect.' Fred lowered his voice and leaned in, 'When no one is looking, we would like you John to surreptitiously make a wax impression of your neighbor's key without getting anyone's notice.'

John and I glanced nervously at each other. We knew, at that moment, this first assignment with the agency had just made our jobs very real. Trying to sound more relaxed than I felt, I asked? 'Do you have a plan?'

Fred smiled and continued talking to put us at ease, 'Tell me a little about the layout of your neighbor's house. Our intel says it should be similar to yours.'

Together, we discussed several scenarios of how we might safely complete this task, and we eventually produced a plan.

We had observed that most of the houses in Nairobi had large old-fashioned skeleton keys with intricate designs on the ends, the kind you might see opening an old treasure chest. Many of our friends kept the keys in the door throughout the day— locking and unlocking as people appeared at their door. We had such a key and because our houses were identical, we were fairly sure that our neighbors had the same set up. At the end of our session with Fred, we felt confident that we had devised a suitable plan to remove the key from the door, complete the task and replace it without getting caught.

When Fred felt no one was paying attention to us, he slid a small metal container with a sliding metal top across the table. 'Open it.'

The small metal box was filled with what looked to be wax. Fred explained. 'When you take the key upstairs, press it down on the wax until it pushes the key firmly into place. Carefully remove the key, slide the box closed and hide it somewhere in your closet until we next meet. Be careful.'

We assured Fred that we would do our best to successfully complete the assignment. Neither of us knew why the CIA wanted the key, and we didn't ask. During this time, we knew that Mohammed's country, along with several other countries, were participating in peace negotiations in the Middle East. As a potential recruit for the agency, we suspected Mohammed might be able to provide insights in the negotiations for the CIA. It was pure speculation on our part.

I saw Babekka the next day and accepted the invitation to the cocktail party and casually mentioned that one of us would be checking on the girls, who would be sleeping upstairs in our apartment. We felt that this was a plausible excuse for leaving the party from time to time without suspicion.

The night of the cocktail party came, and we could see guests arriving and going into Mohammed and Babekka's home. Shauna and Tara were tucked into bed and fast asleep as we prepared to leave our duplex. We were nervous as we made our way downstairs to join the party. Babekka greeted us at the door with a warm smile and introduced us to several other guests. We were relieved to see that their skeleton key was resting in the keyhole of the front door. I tried to remember various names and what the guests did for employment, but my mind raced in nervous anticipation. I was thankful when John brought me a glass of wine. I observed that our Russian neighbor next door, Sergei and his wife, were not in attendance. I decided not to inquire about them.

In a soft voice John whispered that we should mingle with the guests for an hour before he would excuse himself to *check on our daughters* who were sleeping upstairs. Over the past few days, we had discussed the plan for *borrowing* the door key. My job would be to stand near the front door to block the other guests' view of John, as he slipped out the door unnoticed with the proposed key in hand.

The moment arrived, and I knew there was no turning back. John gave me a nod. We both moved to the entrance. I placed my back nearer the door as John stood behind me. I observed the guests socializing in small groups. Lively conversation could be heard throughout the lounge area as guests stood talking with drinks in their hands. Others sat in chairs or on the sofa eating the assortment of offerings from the buffet table. No one seemed focused on the young American couple near the door. I coughed, which signaled that we were being unobserved.

I heard the front door open and click shut. With so many people in attendance, there had been no reason for Mohammed and Babekka to lock the door. I glanced back and observed that the key had slipped unnoticed from the keyhole. I turned around and kept my focus on the party. I nearly dropped my wine glass when I saw Mohammed make his way across the room to chat with me.

'It must be difficult for you to be at a party where you know so few people. Where is that handsome husband of yours?'

I stepped back a little closer to the door and flashed Mohammed a smile. 'John ran upstairs to check on the girls.'

'Ah, I see. I hope you are having an enjoyable time. My wife is an excellent cook. Have you tried any of the items from the buffet table?'

I attempted to keep the appearance of casual conversation. I was petrified that John would return and not be able to replace the key in the door with Mohammed standing so near me. 'Not yet, but as soon as John returns, we plan to get a plate. It smells delicious. I must say I enjoy the aroma of the garlic and spices she makes each day for your lunch.'

'Yes, Babekka is a wonderful cook...' Mohammed continued chatting, but I have no recollection of what he was saying to me. I just smiled and kept nodding my head.

John had been gone for about ten minutes and I wondered how long it would take to make the impression of the key. I knew it would be disastrous if Mohammed chose to stay near the door to keep me company. I took a long sip from my wine glass until it was empty, as Mohammed continued talking about Babekka's cooking.

I looked at my empty glass and said, 'This wine is lovely. Is it produced in your country?'

'No, this particular wine is a Chianti from Tuscany. Babekka and I went there on our honeymoon. Such a beautiful region of Italy. Have you been?'

'No.' I offered.

I let out a sigh of relief when Mohammed asked if he could refresh my glass of wine.

'Moe, that would be so nice of you,' I responded with a relieved smile.

'It is my pleasure, Linda.'

I watched as Mohammed made his way to the drinks table. I prayed I might hear the sound of John come through the front door. Silence.

My heart sank as I saw Mohammed making his way across the room with my glass of wine. Fortunately, luck prevailed when another guest intercepted him halfway.

At that moment I heard the front door open and close. I turned to greet John and was relieved when I glanced down to see the key resting in the keyhole. 'That was nerve-racking,' I whispered. John's face looked pale. All he could do was nod.

Mohammed walked over and asked, 'All is well upstairs, John?' as he handed me the replenished glass of wine.

'Yes. The girls are sound asleep.'

We talked a bit longer with Mohammed until I said, 'John, I'm feeling a bit hungry. Let's allow Moe to mingle with his other guests and we'll get something to eat.'

'Yes, yes. Babekka will be unhappy if you do not try her dishes.'

The rest of the evening was a bit of a blur. The assignment had left us unnerved. But we had accomplished our first mission with the agency and now all we had to do was turn the wax impression over to Fred.

We arranged to get the wax-key duplicator kit to Fred the next day with the imprint of Mohammed and Babekka's key. Then we waited. Weeks went by with no knowledge of why we had been ordered to copy the key. We continued to check the post office boxes and further our friendship with Mohammed and Babekka. It was an easy task as they were a warm and fun-loving couple.

* * * * * *

A few weeks after moving to Hurlingham, John surprised the girls and me by bringing home a white lab rat given to him by the science teacher at NIS. He looked sheepishly at me and said, 'The science teacher said she had an extra rat and thought of the girls.'

Miss Gretchen Pruden had been hired by NIS to teach eighth grade science. 'Gretchen told me she had too many specimens and thought the girls might like to have the little rat as a pet.'

'We love him, Mommy, please let us keep him,' implored Shauna.

Tara, who was petting and cuddling the rat, echoed Shauna's words, 'Yes…PLEASE! I already love him!'

Just before moving from our country cottage in Thika, our little kitten, Posie, had died from a strange sickness. I knew the girls were missing her. I reluctantly gave in and said, 'I will let you keep the rat, but I get to name him.'

'What will it be?' they both chimed.

'I believe we should call him Stilton.'

'What's a Stilton?' asked Tara.

'A Stilton is a type of cheese made in England. And you know how much rats love cheese.'

'I like cheese too,' said Tara speaking directly to the bundle of white fur in her hands.

So, Stilton became a part of the family. We had every intention of getting a cage for the little guy but with money being tight, we kept putting it off. We placed newspaper in the kitchen and Stilton eventually made a nest out of the newsprint and found a permanent home in a corner behind the stove. We placed a bowl of water near the corner wall and fed him out of a shallow bowl, much like a dog or cat.

Often, when I would be doing the dishes at the sink, Stilton would scurry over and lightly raise his little front paws and gently scratch my ankle to remind me that I had forgotten to feed him dinner.

'Ah, Stilton, I completely forgot about you today. Let me get you something for your dinner.' I then would place the offering in a shallow bowl next to his water.

About once a week, our houseboy George would sweep behind the stove, and we would leave fresh newspaper for the rat to shred for his nest. Stilton grew to be fairly fat from living in what must have been rat heaven. He had the run of the house but slept most of the day and rarely ventured past the kitchen unless the girls took him off to their bedroom for playtime.

* * * * * *

After the invitation to Mohammed and Babekka's party, I decided it would be polite to have them up to our apartment for dinner. Fred endorsed the idea. We were pleased when they accepted. The evening was moving along well. I had stuffed thin slices of beef with herbs, rice, and feta cheese, which I served with green beans almondine and salad. Conversation flowed easily as we moved from the dining room table to the sitting area for coffee and dessert. I thought nothing of it when Babekka offered to refill her glass with water from the kitchen sink.

Moments later, we heard a blood-curdling scream which echoed throughout the house, followed by Babekka running out of the kitchen and into the sitting area. John and I looked at each other in horror and exclaimed, 'Stilton!'

Babekka was visibly shaken, and it took us several minutes to explain that Stilton was a family pet. She looked at us like we had lost our minds.

In a shaky voice, Babekka relayed the ordeal. 'I was at the sink getting the water, when all of a sudden, I felt scratching on my leg. I looked down to see this rather large white rat. Well, that is when I screamed.'

In the end, we were able to smooth the incident over, although I recall that no one was laughing. John and I decided that perhaps it was not such a clever idea to let a rat run free in the house. A few days later, I approached our houseboy, George, who had been told about the unfortunate incident with Babekka.

'Kuja hapa, George. Come to the kitchen, I have a favor to ask.'

'Ndio. What is this job, memsahib?'

'George, we think it might be time to give Stilton his independence.'

'Are you certain, memsahib? I have come to grow quite fond of this little rat, but I understand the problem. The other servants who work for the couple downstairs know the story of Memsahib Babekka and Stilton. They found it very amusing.'

Like most people, we learned that Kenyans loved to reveal gossip. 'I think you might have shared this story, George.'

George looked at me and smiled. 'It was very funny.'

'I like Stilton too, but other guests might not understand he's just a pet. I don't think Stilton would be happy with living in a cage after his life of freedom. Therefore, I would like you to take him out to the field behind the property and let him loose. I hope he'll meet up with other rats. All I know is he just can't stay here any longer. I think it would be best to do this when the girls are not around.'

George looked at Stilton who was drinking water from his bowl and nodded. 'Ndio, memsahib. I will do this job for you.'

'Ahsante sana, George.'

Maybe it was out of consideration for my feelings, but George waited until I was busy in another part of the house. Later that day I noticed that the shredded newspaper behind the stove had been swept clean and the little water and food dishes had been removed. It made me a little melancholy.

That evening, we explained to the girls that we thought Stilton was lonely and we sent him on his way to meet others of his kind. They were a little sad, but the incident with the rat was soon forgotten. Babekka was extremely happy when I told her we had gotten rid of the rodent.

Chapter 11:
Sergei and the Soviet *Onion*

One day, arriving home after playing a game of squash at Parklands Social Club, I saw Babekka talking to our Russian neighbor next door. I smiled and gave a friendly wave as I exited my car. Babekka waved back and motioned for me to come over. I wished I had not been wearing tennis gear, but decided this was an opportunity I could not pass up. I cut through a gap in the hedge separating our two properties and walked to where Sergei and Babekka were standing in front of the Russian's two-story house.

I offered a friendly smile and said, 'Hello.'

Babekka's husband, Mohammed, had a particularly good grasp of the English language, but Babekka was not as proficient and occasionally stumbled with words.

'Linda,' Babekka exclaimed with enthusiasm, 'come, come. I would like to introduce you to our good neighbor, Sergei. He is from the Soviet *Onion*.'

Sergei stifled a laugh. I liked Babekka and didn't want her to feel silly or embarrassed that she had misspoken, so I quickly reached out my hand and said, 'It's lovely to meet you, Sergei. I'm your neighbor Linda from the United States of *Asparagus*.'

Sergei paused for a moment, then let out a loud boisterous laugh, which broke the ice. Babekka covered her face and apologized. 'Please, please, you must excuse my English. I say word is *onion* when I mean to say *union*.' Sergei kept laughing and at that moment the two of us bonded like we were old comrades.

Whenever Sergei was *enjoying the air* on his front porch, he usually waved John and me over for a chat, which we were always delighted to do. It was our job to act friendly around him. Sergei was married, but his wife rarely came outside. He apologized for this and said she didn't speak English.

In the course of our visits, Sergei asked us casual questions as to why we were in Nairobi. We found it easy to answer him truthfully and tell him about our connection with Nairobi International School. John kept the conversation light and talked of coaching, rugby, and his love of fly fishing.

Relations between the United States and the Soviet Union had been deteriorating since WWII with the takeover of much of Europe in what Winston Churchill called Russia's Iron Curtain. In the early 1960s, tensions had escalated between President John Kennedy and Nikita Khrushchev during the Cuban Missile Crisis. The icy relationship warmed a little in the early 1970s. Under the leadership of Leonid Brezhnev, the Soviet regime proclaimed a policy of détente, seeking economic cooperation and disarmament negotiations with the West. Despite the proclamation, everyone knew that the Cold War was in full force.

We knew from Fred that Sergei was a likely KGB operative. He was a proud Communist through and through. In the early seventies we were at the height of the Cold War. The Iron Curtain dominated the tensions between our two countries. Often, in conversations, Sergei would steer us in the direction of nationalism.

'I have been to America and although there are things I admire about your country; I must say that I have a huge problem with your Mafia.'

John and I looked at each other with a blank stare. John offered, 'Well, I know there was a problem in the thirties during Prohibition. I've not heard much about the Mafia today.'

'Oh no, my friends. Your country has *too much problem* with the Mafia. I am proud to say that we have no Mafia in the Soviet Union. It would not be tolerated.'

He then continued on about the evils of all the groups of Mafia in the US. We listened but didn't challenge him or offer our views on the subject. Our job was to portray ourselves as a young couple with little interest in government or politics.

Sergei seemed really passionate about this and brought up the subject numerous times. 'That is one thing that is better in my country. We do not have any Mafia gangs like you do in your country. I think your government should do something about this.'

John and I never challenged him on his views on the American Mafia problem. We followed Howard and Fred's admonitions to play the part of a pair of young twenty-somethings out of touch with world politics. We were coached to act surprised and a little disturbed when we heard him talk about the *little things* he considered big problems for the average American. We were instructed never to challenge him with what we considered might be wrong with the Soviet Union. For all we knew, Sergei might have been trying to recruit us.

We loved living in Kenya, but when living abroad there is a longing for home and an inclination of pride for one's country—a need to follow current events. Therefore, unlike the persona we portrayed to Sergei, John and I were actually very informed with political and social affairs happening in the United States. It helped us stay connected to the country we loved. In Nairobi, we did not have a television, and evenings could be long. Each week, we bought and read *Time* and *Newsweek* magazines, as well as the *International Herald Tribune* from cover to cover. Each month, I reviewed the *New York Times* bestselling books and read most of them. It's amazing how productive one can be without watching TV. Sometimes, Howard Bane would loan the rugby club a 16-millimeter film and a projector to watch American football highlights. He also provided the projector for sporting events, like the New Zealand All Blacks rugby game. We and our British friends looked forward to these events, which helped connect us with home.

Sergei appeared to be in his late forties or early fifties but from my twenty-six-year-old perspective, he looked old. He had gray hair and was a little overweight, which he carried in his belly. I had the suspicion that Sergei had a slight crush on me. He seemed eager to engage me in conversation and would often wave me over for a chat. I didn't flirt with him, but I laughed at his jokes and never made him feel like a foolish older man. His advances were harmless enough and we were doing the job we had signed up for.

One day he announced that he would soon be leaving Kenya to go on home leave in Russia. I told him to enjoy his family. He surprised me by saying, 'We have many beautiful things in my country. I will enjoy bringing you several gifts upon my return in a month.'

I thanked him and told him it wasn't necessary, but he waved me off with his hand.

We passed this information on to Fred, who seemed excited upon learning this. During this meeting, Fred gave us the key the CIA had made with the wax impression of our Middle Eastern neighbors' front door, and he instructed us to look for an opportunity to *test* it.

'Don't take any chances, but we need you to verify if the key works on the door.'

John nodded his head and placed the key back in its envelope.

'Keep it hidden in a safe place in your bedroom.' John affirmed that he would.

'Fred, a few days ago, I was having tea with Babekka, and she mentioned that their family would be away this coming weekend visiting friends in Limuru. Perhaps we should test it then.'

Fred said, 'This is a fantastic opportunity, Linda. Let's make it happen.'

LEADING A DOUBLE LIFE—Tara's birthday party at the Hurlingham duplex. Our upstairs apartment is out of frame. The door to the left of the porch is where we *tested* the duplicate key of our Middle Eastern neighbors. The suspected KGB Russian operative, Sergei's house is to the left past the low hedge and is also out of frame—1973

Making *it happen* was easier said than done. Our two-story duplex sat away from the street with a large area for parking and a large grass lawn. However, it would be easy for people to peer into the property. Although the street we lived on was in a suburb of Nairobi called Hurlingham, the streets were often crowded with pedestrians. Most Kenyans walked, rode bikes, or enjoyed public transportation. Very few of the locals could afford the luxury of owning a car. People seemed to be everywhere that Sunday. Plus, although Mohammed's family was gone for the weekend, their houseboy and his family were still on the property. At the moment, they were in their servant's quarters behind the house. We feared they might take a walk by or come to the front of the property. We were nervous.

John and I lingered near Mohammed's porch on the pretense of watching our girls having a tea party with their dolls on a blanket, which I had spread on the grass. My job was to make sure the pedestrians were not peering into the property and to warn John if Mohammed's houseboy came out front.

I gave John a nod when the foot traffic abated. John casually ventured up the porch to our neighbor's door and thrust the key into the lock. I waited for him to come back down the steps, and wondered why he was taking so long. Minutes flew by, and my face grew warm as my heart rate quickened. *Why is he taking so long?*

Finally, John walked down the steps and approached me with a stricken look on his face. My heart sank. I knew something had gone wrong. 'What happened?'

'We have a huge problem, Linda. I had no difficulty inserting the key into the lock. I was even able to unlock it and open the front door. I turned the key into the lock position, but now I can't get the key to come out. It's stuck and it will not dislodge!'

'You've got to be joking. What are you going to do?'

'I don't know. I tried, but the key just won't budge for me. I think you should give it a shot. Perhaps a woman's touch?' he offered with little confidence. 'All I know, if our neighbors come home and see a strange key jammed into their front door, we're toast. Our cover will be completely blown.'

I nodded. My heart was beating fast, and my mouth had gone dry, but I knew we couldn't leave the key in the door. I looked at John and said, 'I'll try.'

John became the lookout man, and I ventured up the steps to the front door. I looked at the key for a few seconds and decided to approach the problem differently. I deduced that perhaps John was trying to muscle the key to get it out of the lock. I chose to try a more delicate approach. My hands were shaking as I gently wiggled the key back and forth trying to feel it click into the correct chambers. It took a while, and I was beginning to give up hope when the key began to dislodge from its cavity. I let out a sigh of relief when the key finally released itself and was firmly grasped in my hand. I checked to make sure the door was locked and retreated down the stairs. My face was beet red as I nodded to John and slowly opened my palm.

'How did you do that?'

'I just willed it to come out, I guess. I kept gently moving the key back and forth without forcing it.'

'Next question. Is the door open or locked?'

'I jiggled the handle before I left and thankfully the door is in the locked position.'

I think, at that moment, what we really needed was a stiff drink. Instead, we gathered the girls from their tea party on the blanket and asked, 'Who would like to go into town and get a soft-serve ice cream at the shop.'

'Ice cream, yes, yes,' they squealed.

* * * * * *

People have asked us if we ever felt our lives were in danger when working undercover for the CIA. I never felt we were ever in imminent danger. But there were dangerous incidents, like that of the stuck key. What was unpleasant for us was leading a double life. There were times when we had to lie to our friends and family so as to not blow our cover. It often felt like a betrayal.

While living in the duplex, we had an agent from Washington come to our home for training purposes. He had been with us for several hours and it was getting dark. We were finishing up our session when we heard the downstairs doorbell ring. John looked confused as we were not expecting guests. He went to see who it was. I stiffened when I heard the voices of our Harlequin friends Dougie and Margaret Hamilton echo up the stairwell.

'We were in the area and thought we'd stop by for a visit. Hope that's okay?'

John felt it would seem strange to turn our friends away, and suddenly we heard the sound of their shoes as they ascended the stairs.

The agent looked unnerved and said, 'I don't want to meet anyone.'

'I'm sorry about this, and I completely understand.'

I ushered the agent into the bathroom and told him to wait. 'When we get our friends situated in the living room, John will escort you through the hall and down the stairs. I will produce an excuse as to why you are here.' My head was spinning with a plausible reason for having a guest in our home who did not want to meet our friends.

John seated Dougie and Margaret in the lounge and went to find me. 'I'll get Linda.'

John met me in the hallway. 'Linda, where did he go?'

'He's in the bathroom,' I whispered. 'He's a little unnerved and does not want to be introduced. I'll engage our guests while you escort him through the hall and down the stairs.'

I tried to make easy conversation, but our friends knew something was amiss, and they watched in confusion as John hustled a strange man out of the house.

'Who was that?' asked Margaret. 'That was quite strange.'

'Doesn't your visitor want to meet us?' questioned Dougie.

'I saw a car parked downstairs, but assumed it was for your downstairs neighbors.'

'Maybe we've come at a bad time.'

Dougie and Margaret's banter was a blessing and gave me a moment to produce a believable story as to why we did not introduce the illusive visitor to them.

'I'm deeply sorry about that. That man is a teacher at NIS. Unfortunately, he was terribly upset. He's having marital trouble and thinks his wife might be cheating on him. He came over for advice. He was extremely distressed and didn't want to talk to anyone.'

John came back upstairs and gathered a bottle of wine and four glasses from the dining room cupboard. He had been listening to my excuse and joined in the charade. 'He's not himself. We hope you understand.' I inwardly smiled at the irony of John's words.

Dougie made several jokes about our shy guest skulking out of the house. Margaret had to be reassured they were not imposing. I'm not sure they bought the lie, but we kept on with the ruse and eventually the conversation switched to another topic.

Living a double life could be challenging and that challenge became even harder when my parents, Bruce and Esther, would eventually come for a second visit to Kenya in 1974.

Chapter 12:
1972 – Two Bugging Operations

Throughout the next few weeks, Fred and Howard told us that a series of American agents would be arriving at our house. We didn't know if they worked for the embassy or came from outside the country. They introduced themselves by their first names and very little chitchat followed. They were efficient and upon completing their assigned tasks left quickly and without fanfare. The agents came to instruct us how to pass information without looking suspicious, and how to take clandestine photos, known as hip shots, with the Pentax camera on loan to us from the CIA.

One agent gave us a stern lecture when I mentioned we were part-time agents. 'Working for the CIA is never part time. It is full-time, and you are always on the job, always alert to what's happening around you, always conscious of your undercover status while making observations. Remember, it is not just your husband working for us, Linda. You too must be aware of your surroundings and assist in every situation. You will have a unique perspective on assignments, so use it.'

We were shown how to take a photo from the waist, called a *hip shot*, from the 35-millimeter Pentax, to capture an image of a target without their knowledge. The agents were extremely professional, and only spoke to us to explain how to operate a piece of machinery or where to store a CIA item. We had one clothes closet and a series of two large cabinets in our master bedroom. Two men wired electricity to the inside of a large cabinet and installed a large reel to reel tape recorder. They fixed a lock to the outside of the cabinet door that could only be opened with a key. We assumed it was secured so our house servant would not be able to open the cupboard when we were gone. Extra tapes were stored inside the cabinet.

Fred told us that two of our jobs were to bug the Russian's house next door and our Middle Eastern neighbors below us. We knew nothing as to the specific details of the operations.

I had mixed feelings about recording Mohammed and Babekka. They were lovely people, and our children played together. I knew they were friendly with the Russian, Sergei. I assumed that the CIA had their reasons, so I tried not to think about it as a betrayal.

I had grown especially fond of Babekka, and we often visited each other over coffee or tea. Babekka was also friendly with a European model named Anya. When Anya wasn't away on a modeling job, she lived with her art dealer boyfriend in Nairobi. Anya was as thin as a pole and once told me she had to eat a large bar of Cadbury chocolate each day to keep her weight up. I remember being envious of this fact. Even though I was in my mid-twenties, I worked at watching my weight. I had always loved sports and played on my high school volleyball team. With the ability to have help in Nairobi, I was able to jog, play squash, tennis, golf, and swim to stay in shape. Anya just had one of those lucky metabolisms.

Babekka was very exotic looking. She loved to wear heavy face makeup and style her long ebony hair in fancy intricate patterns. Her black eyes were her most dramatic feature. She outlined them with heavy eyeliner and mascara, and smoothed rich hues of blue and green eyeshadow in the style of Cleopatra. No matter the time of day, I never saw her without paint on her face. Babekka was always pestering me to allow her to practice her skills on me.

'You are such a pretty young woman, Linda. You have lovely blue eyes. You should wear makeup. Why don't you allow me to give you a lesson on how to apply color to enhance your eyes? I will call on my friend Anya and we will make you look beautiful. Your husband will not recognize you.'

I have never worn foundation makeup and usually just put a little mascara on my eye lashes and blush on my cheeks. I reluctantly agreed to let Babekka and Anya have a go with me. I considered it as part of doing my bit for Uncle Sam.

Several days later, I met Anya and Babekka downstairs in her apartment. I sat in a kitchen chair and let them use my face as their canvas. The kitchen table was ladened with more makeup than I had even seen. I was not allowed to look in a mirror. I suppose they wanted the *reveal* to be a surprise. Forty minutes later they stood back smiling. Babekka thrust a mirror into my hand. When I finally looked at my image, I did not recognize the woman staring back at me. I felt as though I looked like a clown, but Babekka and Anya kept telling me how beautiful I was. I smiled and tried to be as gracious as my feelings would allow. My eyes had been dramatically painted with coal black eyeliner and heavily applied blue and green eye shadow. I thought I looked like an extra in the movie *Cleopatra.*

I never left the house for the rest of the day and waited for John to come home so I could clean the makeup off my face. I thought John would collapse on the floor, he laughed so hard. I stormed into the bathroom and spent the next fifteen minutes applying tons of cotton balls to remove the layers of paint. I knew Babekka was sad the next time she saw me looking plain and drab.

She asked, 'How did your husband like the way you looked?'

'Although John has always liked me to have a more natural look, he thought I looked quite beautiful. I really appreciate what you did for me. I promise to apply what you taught me when we have a formal night out.' Babekka seemed to be satisfied that her tutorial had not been in vain.

A week later, I ran into Anya at the market, and she pulled me aside.

'I think you did not like the way we made up your face.' I looked at her but said nothing. 'Personally, I think Babekka went a little overboard with the paint. I would have gone a little more subtle.'

'That style of makeup looks wonderful on Babekka with her olive skin and exotic features. I'm of Irish descent with light skin and freckles. I just don't feel I can pull that look off. But she has such a sweet nature, and I hope that I didn't hurt her feelings.'

'She will understand.'

In my mind I was reflecting, *There is a line in the sand that needs to be drawn...even for Uncle Sam!*

Throughout this period, we were still socializing with the Bane family. We were often invited for dinner or cocktails. On one occasion, I mentioned that I would love to return the favor and have them both over to our home for dinner.

Howard sipped on his martini and said, 'I think we could make this happen, but, for security reasons, we would have to park our car away from your property and be picked up.'

'There's a small market on New Caledonian Street a few blocks from our house,' offered John. 'I think that would be a safe place to leave your car. It's near the President's State House and there's a lot of police activity in the area.' We set a date for an evening at our house. The parking issue worked out that evening and it was decided that this would be the plan for future dinner parties at our home.

A few weeks later Fred invited us over to his house for a meeting, which he did on occasion to collect mail from the post office boxes and gather intel updates from us.

'Fred, Babekka said that she and Mohammed will be spending a week up at Molo.'

'Yes. We already know this.'

I was surprised and wondered how he already knew this information, but let it pass. I wondered if another operative working undercover for the CIA had invited them for the week. If the embassy had somehow extended the invitation, we never knew. We were rapidly learning that everything we did was on a strictly need-to-know basis.

Fred lowered his voice to a whisper. 'The CIA will be conducting two clandestine entry operations simultaneously next week, and we will be using your house as a staging area and listening post. Howard says that the market on New Caledonian Street has been used to leave his vehicle, for safety and security, when he and Anita have visited you socially.'

We nodded in the affirmative.

'We will be parking a few cars in that same spot and will arrange with another intelligence service to keep an eye on them for us.'

I was a little confused when Fred mentioned the involvement of another intelligence service, but it all became clear to us as the operation unfolded.

'Your job, John, will be to pick us up in your van at the market off New Caledonian Street. There will be four or five of us involved. We will gather inside your residence before the operation. You two will stay inside your house. When the job is completed, we will meet back at your house, and you will deliver us back to the market. For your information, we will be placing listening devices in the Middle Eastern couple below you and the Russian KGB operative next door to you.'

I knew that Sergei and his wife had gone to Russia on home leave. 'How will you enter Sergei's house?' I asked. John and I had only copied the key to our downstairs neighbor's house, but as yet had not known that a second listening device would be installed there.

'Leave that problem to us.'

We agreed to make sure the girls would be asleep and to give our houseboy the day off in the hopes that he would use the time to take the bus into the city to see a movie.

The night of the operation came, and John made the pickup at 11:00 PM. Ten minutes later, Howard, Fred, and three other men we had never seen before came up the stairs and entered our lounge. They were completely dressed in black cotton pants and black turtleneck jerseys. Black knitted stocking caps, shoes, and gloves completed their outfits. I remember thinking at the time, *Gee, this is just like the movies.* It was a surreal moment for me.

We were not invited to be a part of the actual operation and were instructed to stay at the house until the team returned, at which time John would transport the men back to the loading area.

A signal was given. The men quietly exited the house, and we waited. It's difficult to remember how long they were gone, but I seemed like hours. The girls slept peacefully in their beds while John and I tried to read, but mostly stared at each other in nervous anticipation. At length, the men quietly entered our house and remained in the stairwell. Howard came upstairs and motioned for John to escort the men back to the area where they had parked their vehicle.

John was back in fifteen minutes. I looked at him and said, 'That was something I never expected to be a part of.'

'They were very efficient. Did you hear them downstairs in Mohammed's house?'

'No. And I was listening. I'm glad the key worked.'

We later learned from Howard who the other intelligence service was that participated in the operation. It came as an interesting surprise, but one I will not share here for security reasons. We were never told how the team was able to enter

Sergei's house undetected and install a listening device somewhere in his residence.

After the success of installing the listening devices, our instructions were to record the Russian's house anytime we noticed that he was having a dinner party or any company over to his house. The same applied to our downstairs neighbors. However, we were instructed that the Russian bugging operation would take precedence in the off chance that both assets were entertaining on the same night.

Each night we would check to see if there was any unusual activity or different cars parked in front of the Russian's house. If so, we would activate the reel-to-reel tape recorder, adjust the volume, and press record.

Naturally, the conversations at Sergei's house were in Russian, so we had no idea what was being said. We would then pass the tapes off to Fred, who told us they would be sent to Washington to be analyzed. We were never told anything beyond that.

I suspected that Sergei had a bit of a crush on me, but as a young girl in my twenties, I thought of him as a less attractive version of my dad. I found him to be less flirtatious when John and I were invited to sit on his porch together for a chat. During those times, he continued to regale us with the merits of the *motherland* and slip subtle hints of why we should be suspicious of Mafia elements rampant in the US. I'm sure he must have thought we were either naïve or foolish. We never challenged him on any of his views. He sometimes asked what we thought about the Kennedy assassination or whether we liked Richard Nixon. He was very interested in the Watergate scandal, which he considered a further indication that there was corruption in our government. Our purpose was to allow him to believe that maybe we considered that there might be some truth to his ramblings. We were instructed to portray ourselves as a young couple in their twenties who were not the least bit interested in political affairs.

One afternoon arriving home from a round of squash at Parklands Club, I saw Sergei motioning for me to come over for a visit. I hadn't seen him since his return from Russia. He waved for me to come over to where he stood near his front porch. I was nervous as I passed through the hedge which separated our properties and waved hello. I worried that he somehow suspected that a listening device had been placed in his house while he was gone. I forced a smile as I closed the gap between us.

'Greetings, my American friend.'

'How are you, Sergei? I hope you had a good vacation at home in Russia. Did you see family?'

'Yes, yes, of course, but I'm happy to be back in Nairobi. Please stay here. I have some gifts for you that I brought from Russia.' I felt a little uncomfortable walking up the steps to the porch knowing that Sergei's wife was inside. We had never been invited inside Sergei's house, and I rarely ever had contact with his elusive wife. I followed him up the porch steps and stood near a chair waiting for Sergei to return. Sergei came out his front door moments later and closed it behind him. 'Come, come, Linda. Sit on the porch with me. It would bring me pleasure to watch you open the parcels.'

I was a bit taken aback that Sergei had followed through and actually did bring us something while he was away in Russia. I smiled and nodded as he pointed for me to sit in one of the chairs. I breathed a sigh of relief that nothing seemed unusual in our first meeting since his return from Russia. There was no indication that he suspected that a listening device had been placed inside his house. Sergei held three packages wrapped in plain brown paper. He was beaming with pride as he pressed the gifts into my hands.

'Sergei, this is truly kind of you. Do you want me to open them here?'

'Yes, yes.'

I gathered the packages and began to open two smaller wrapped items.

'These first two are for your little daughters.'

The first package I opened revealed a beautifully painted stack of Matryoshka (sometimes called Babushka) dolls in the traditional style of dress and scarf of a peasant woman. The second package was the same doll but in different colors.

Sergei smiled and said, 'The proper Russian word for these wooden dolls is *matryoshka.* Smaller dolls are hidden inside the one in your hand. Open it and see.'

Carefully, I opened the largest doll and was delighted to see a similar, but slightly smaller doll resting inside the hollow cavity. I continued until there were five dolls in assorted sizes and colors on my lap. The last little doll could not be opened. 'Sergei, the girls will be delighted with these lovely gifts. I carefully rewrapped the two sets of nesting dolls for the girls to open. 'Thank you for thinking of my girls. I know they will love them.'

'The dolls are made from lime wood or birch. The craftsman turns the wood on a lathe and then chisels the interior to make the dolls hollow. It has been done in our country for years. The work is tedious, but Russian winters can be long, so I think it was something for the wood carver to fill his time during the long winter nights. Some people incorrectly call them babushka dolls, but this word is not exactly right. Babushka means grandmother in Russian.'

'Again, thank you. It was exceedingly kind of you to think of us.'

'The next one is for you,' he voiced with pride.

I unwrapped a larger package in brown paper and saw a large shawl with an exquisite print of red and yellow roses and green leaves on a black background. The shawl was woven and exceptionally soft, although I was not certain of its material. It was bordered with red tassels forming a fringe around the edge. To my twenty-six-year-old mind, I thought the shawl looked like something my grandmother might wear. Looking back, I wish I would have had the foresight to keep the shawl because the workmanship was outstanding. I did not appreciate the shawl at the time, and I felt a little uncomfortable taking the gift. I stumbled for a moment not knowing quite what to say. I gathered myself and said, 'Sergei, this is beautiful.'

'Put it on. It is to be worn around the shoulders on a cool night or sitting by the fire in your house in the winter. I smiled and thought as I wrapped the shawl around my shoulders, *Have you been to California, Sergei?*

I could not imagine ever wearing the shawl but said, 'Again, thank you for your kindness in thinking of us.'

Sergei had no gift for John. I thought this to be a little unusual, but John waved it off as nothing. 'He always seemed to prefer your company to mine.'

Chapter 13:
December 1972
Fishing and Fishers of Men

John and I had made friends with a Catholic family who were working in Kenya. Doc Gilbert and his wife Josie were almost finished with a two-year stint in Nairobi. Doc was on loan as a veterinarian and had a practice in town. They had a large family but only their younger children joined them in Kenya and were attending Nairobi International School. Doc Gilbert had assisted us when our cat Posie got sick and helped us put her down.

The Gilberts asked us to go camping with them at Lake Turkana in the northwestern section of the Kenya Rift Valley. We were enjoying another Christmas break during our second year in Nairobi. They wanted us to meet two Catholic missionary priests from Ireland working in Eldoret. The priests were planning to visit and bring supplies to other missionary priests and nuns working to help Turkana tribes living in the dry arid northern district of Kenya. The Gilberts and we offered to carry an assortment of supplies in our Volkswagen buses.

Lake Turkana was also a favorite stop for tourists who were interested in fishing the large Nile Perch that inhabited the alkaline lake. Nile Perch are one of the largest freshwater fish and can grow to almost seven feet in length and weigh over three hundred pounds and are considered quite the catch for avid fishermen. Nile Perch are fierce predators and feed on crustaceans, mollusks, and insects, but the fish are vulnerable to larger predators inhabiting the lake, such as crocodiles. The richer tourists flew by small planes into the region to cast their lures and snare the large silver fish. We were planning on driving overland through three hundred miles of rough washboard dirt roads and stopping at the various missions along the way to visit the priests and nuns who were serving the Turkana people.

Like our safari to Mombasa, we took the back seat out and made a bed for us while we camped. The bus would become our home for the next ten days. We left Nairobi early in the morning and descended down the eastern escarpment and crossed the Rift Valley. We climbed up the western escarpment and stopped off in the town of Eldoret where we would spend the night before heading north to Lake Turkana in the morning.

We followed the Gilberts into the parking lot of a Baptist Church. Doc explained, 'We have been invited to dinner by a veterinarian friend of mine who attends this Baptist church. Then we will head on over to the Catholic Church where we will bunk for the night.'

We were introduced to Doc's friend and his family and were treated to a lovely buffet supper hosted by the ladies of their church. We filled our plates and sat at a long picnic-style table with others from the congregation.

The drive to Eldoret had been long, and I had the feeling John wanted to relax with a drink. Once seated, John leaned over and whispered, 'Where's the wine?'

To which I whispered, 'Honey, they're Baptists. They don't drink alcohol.'

John looked dejected but nodded his head and continued eating his dinner. After the meal and a visit, Doc thanked his friend, and we said our goodbyes. We followed the Gilberts over to St. John Catholic church in the center of Eldoret.

Upon exiting our vehicles, Doc said, 'Father Patrick Scanlon and young Father Terry Nash are missionary priests from Ireland. Josie and I met Father Scanlon when he was posted in Denver for a short period. They run things at the church here in town.'

We walked into the priest's rectory and were greeted by Father Terry Nash. Father Pat was engaged in an animated conversation on the phone with a parishioner. Father Scanlon had dark hair infused with a smattering of gray. He looked to be somewhere in his mid-forties. Father Terry, a handsome young priest in his mid-twenties, invited us to sit down in their parlor.

At length Father Pat got off the phone and shook his head and said in a broad Irish brogue. 'That Mrs. Barkley is the bane of my existence! But enough of church business. Welcome to our humble home. Now, Father Terry and I have taken a vow of not imbibing of the drink, but we have a delightful selection of wine and whiskey. Might we offer you a beverage to wash away the dust from your travels.'

John smiled and looking at me whispered, 'Now, *these* are my people.' Little did he know that his words would soon have a deeper meaning than he may have intended.

The next morning, we gathered to make the long trek north through the semi-arid desert to camp at Lake Turkana. Father Scanlon and Father Nash were joining us and would be bringing various supplies to their missionary companions. The priests had mapped out several missionary stops along the way. Father Pat offered a blessing for a safe journey, and all three cars were on a washboard dirt road that shook us in the old green bus.

The view outside the window of the bus was a sight to behold. Wild camels and donkeys roamed the arid region and seemed to be everywhere. Mounds of red earth vaulted out of the land and shot up twenty feet in the air. They looked like the wet sandcastles we used to make into towers at the beach by dropping the sand and water mixture from our hands.

When we stopped for a break, Shauna asked Father Terry, 'What are the little sandcastles used for?'

Father Nash explained. 'They may look like wee sandcastles from a distance, but if you get up close you would see that they are giant termite hives, Shauna. It takes years for these termite mounds to form and grow. Thousands of insects live inside. The termites fly out of dirt mounds when it rains and are attracted to light. The Turkana and other tribes love to eat them as a source of protein.'

'How do they do that?' asked Shauna as she wrinkled her nose.

'After they are caught and die, the tribal people pick them up and bite off the end of their torso—you know an insect's bottom.'

'That's gross!'

'Actually Shauna, I have tried one and they do not taste that bad.'

'What did the termite taste like?' asked Tara.

'Well, Tara, it tasted a lot like peanut butter.'

Tara knitted her brow and finally said, 'I like peanut butter, but I don't think I would like a peanut butt.' We laughed at her child-like assessment of the termite's protein.

**Shauna—age three. Sitting on a
termite mound in Turkana.**

We had been traveling for a little over a hundred miles when the old bus came to a sudden standstill. John and Doc were not certain what the problem was, but Father Pat said, 'Now never you mind. 'Tis not a problem. The priest at our mission in Lodwar is a crackerjack mechanic. I'm certain he'll be able to sort out the problem.'

'The priest is a mechanic?' asked John.

'Of course. Living in the middle of nowhere, the priests and nuns have to be able to sort out all kinds of issues to be able to survive in this arid region of Kenya.'

Doc Gilbert said, 'I'll hitch a rope to our car, and we will tow you into the next mission.'

For the second time on one of our trips in the old green bus, we were being pulled along the washboard road in hot and dusty conditions. The Gilberts offered to let the girls ride in their bus. The heat and the dust engulfed the car, and I was happy that my daughters were not breathing in the choking dirt from the road. Several times we had to stop and tie the rope, which broke from time to time due to the jarring motion of the road.

At one point, John had grown very frustrated and jokingly announced to everyone, 'If we ever make it to Lake Turkana, I think I'll *have* to become Catholic because if this bus makes it, it's sure to be a miracle.'

We all laughed and continued on our journey.

We eventually arrived at the mission in Lodwar, where one of the Irish priests began working on the old green bus inside an open-air garage. Another Irish priest showed us around the compound and school and gave us a lesson on what the church was trying to do for the Turkana people.

'The land for these poor souls 'tis harsh, to be sure. They have accepted our help to a degree, but cling to the ancient ways of their tribe. They love to skirmish with their neighbors to steal their cattle or goats and show off their prowess as warriors. Many a night they come into the infirmary covered in blood. We try and patch up their cuts and wounds as best as we can, but sometimes they die. We have one priest who is a doctor and several nuns who assist him in the field of nursing.'

Doc Gilbert asked, 'The land seems so harsh. What do they eat?'

''Tis a problem for sure. Now, the lake is loaded with fish, but for many of the Turkana, fish are considered taboo. We have tried to encourage them to see the value in eating fish. Often, the children are malnourished. The fish from the lake could give them all the protein they need, but it's been hard to encourage them to eat the darn things.

'They live off wild grasses and berries and drink the blood from their cattle. They will kill a goat to eat, but like the Masai, they bleed the cattle for protein and will only eat the flesh of their cattle for special celebrations. They are experts at catching and training camels which roam the area.'

I was interested in the school and asked, 'Has the schooling of the children been a success?'

'The school has been one of our better successes. The children seem eager to learn, and they love to sing. We have another building, which we call our crafts center. It has become an area of learning for the women. We are teaching them to use a sewing machine to sew cloth napkins and other goods, which we sell in Nairobi to the tourists. They make beautiful baskets which we also sell in Nairobi. The baskets and cloth items generate an income for them.

'We have also dug a well and are experimenting with several varieties of citrus trees and a few nut trees.' He showed us the well and some scraggly varieties of trees that looked as though they were struggling to survive.

Our group was invited into the nuns' compound where we were offered cookies from a large tin and steaming cups of hot tea. I thought that a cold drink would have been a better choice until one of the nuns, Sister Andrea, explained.

'Now, you might think 'tis odd to be drinking hot tea on a hot day, but we have found that the tea actually helps cool the body down and is really quite refreshing.'

I was a little surprised that after consuming my cup of tea I felt less warm.

We lingered at Lodwar for several hours and unloaded some of the supplies intended for that mission. The bus was repaired, although I never knew exactly what the problem had been, and we were on our way. I soon grew weary from the monotonous ride. There was no relief from the jarring of the washboard road, and I prayed that we would arrive at the lake with the bus still running.

Lake Turkana, recently renamed from the British Colonial period as Lake Rudolf, was a sight to behold. We were so hot and dusty that the first thing we wanted to do was take a dip in the lake. The ranger that took our money to use the camping area warned us.

'Bwana, you must be very watchful with the little mtotos. Your girls would make a tasty snack for a large crocodile. There are many crocodiles and hippopotamuses in this lake. We have had several mishaps this past year with those who have been injured or have been dragged under by the crocodiles to drown. The crocodiles can only move their jaws up and down, making it hard to eat fresh meat. They pull their prey into the lake where they drown and wedge them under a rock or a branch to rot. It is only then that they can pull and eat the flesh of their victims.'

I cringed at this method of hunting and was reminded of seeing a young boy at Parkland's swimming pool with terrible scars on his torso. I asked Jan Ellis, and she relayed the story of she and John and Gill and Tony Glover who were visiting Buffalo Springs. 'The young lad was snatched from the shore by a crocodile and was slowly being pulled into the water. John and I, along with Tony and Gill Glover, rushed to the boy's aid and with others formed a human chain to thwart the croc from pulling him under. Nothing was working until Gill grabbed a large panga knife and repeatedly hit the crocodile on the head until it finally released its mighty jaws from the boy's torso. The family got lucky because a nurse was there, and she directed the group to flush the gashes with water to halt infection. The Flying Doctors were contacted and flew the boy and his parents to Nairobi for surgery and masses of antibiotics to halt infection.'

I was brought back to the present when the ranger continued. 'The hippos are just as dangerous. They are nocturnal and like to come ashore at night. They will charge a man if they feel you are encroaching on their eating grounds.'

I vowed that the girls and I would ***not*** be going into the lake. That promise, however, was soon broken. It was so hot that we found the only way to get relief was to take a dip in the alkaline waters of the lake. I would caution the girls to stay on the shore while I waded in up to my waist. I would dip into the sea for a few seconds and quickly wade back to shore. I then stood in the water and scanned the shallows for crocs. I let the girls play in the shallows until my nerves got the better of me. We went into the lake many times a day, but it was never a relaxing experience.

The next day, Doc, Josie, and John rented three spots on one of the tourist boats to catch the famed Nile Perch in the lake. They got lucky and caught several mid-sized, but still hefty, perch, which were immediately put on ice.

John explained the system. 'The operators of the boat quickly gutted and skinned the fish. They told us that we would be able to take a portion of the frozen fish home, but it might not be the ones we actually caught. We told them to keep most of our fish, so we were told that our fish dinner tonight would be free.'

'Did you see any hippos on the lake?'

'We did.' John lowered his voice. 'Something happened that was a little embarrassing. I had a bit of a stomach issue and had to go to the bathroom. I mean I *really* had to go. I told Doc that I was going to get in the water to take care of the issue. So, I went to the back of the boat and jumped in. I quickly stripped my swimsuit off and…well, did my business. Doc did a good job keeping Josie and another lady at the front of the boat. It was several nervous minutes for me, but I made it out of the lake and back on the boat without running into a hippo or a croc. Other than that, it was a rewarding fishing safari.'

I laughed as he told the story and was relieved that he didn't get hurt.

We had been camping for two days when John approached me and said, 'I'm going to become a Catholic!"

I was stunned and just a little annoyed. John and his family had never been members of an organized church. When he asked me to marry him, he followed all the protocol for young Catholic couples wanting to marry in the late sixties. He agreed to participate in the Pre-Cana classes, which were mandatory for young couples. He and I met with my parish priest and signed papers promising that John would raise our children as Catholics.

Our marriage bans were announced on the three preceding Sundays at all the Masses to ensure that there was nothing nefarious about one of us that needed an explanation. After we married, John taught PE and coached at Saint Patrick's Grammar School in North Park. He often attended Mass with me and the girls. But, not once had we ever had a deep and meaningful discussion on him being led by the power of the Holy Spirit to become a Catholic.

I looked at him and shook my head. 'John, what do you mean you're going to become a Catholic. You've never mentioned anything like this to me. This seems to be coming out of nowhere!'

He looked at me sheepishly and said, 'Well, remember when I said that if the old bus made it to Lake Turkana, I would have to become a Catholic because it would be a miracle?'

'Yes. You were making a joke.'

'Well, I guess Father Terry and Father Pat saw an opportunity to bring a lost sheep into the fold, because when we stopped at the Lodwar mission, they got the holy oil, salt, and water for the ceremony.' John smiled awkwardly and shrugged his shoulders.

'This is important to me, John, and I wouldn't want you doing this if it's just on a whim. Of course, I have always hoped that with your family not belonging to a church that you might choose to become a Catholic. But this is out of the blue. You told me you were going to become a Catholic like saying you were going to buy a new pair of shoes. It seems a bit cavalier.'

'No, Linda. It's not. I think it would be the best thing for our family. I've been around the priests and nuns when I coached at St. Patrick's. I've come to appreciate your faith.'

'Are you sure you just don't want to hurt Father Pat and Father Terry's feelings?'

'No. I want to do this. Come on and bring your guitar. They're waiting for us in one of the open-air cabañas. Father Terry thought it would be nice if we all sang a song.'

Fifteen minutes later, John was baptized, and Josie and Doc became his godparents. Within the space of thirty minutes, I became the wife of a Catholic. After the sacramental ceremony, I grabbed my guitar, and we all sang *He's Got the Whole World in His Hands* to mark the moment.

Years later, John liked to tell an ameliorated version of the story of his baptism to friends and family. He glorified the moment telling all who would listen how his baptism was a complete immersion in Lake Turkana, with crocodiles and hippos circling near him. He said it was the power of the Lord that kept him safe. I'm not sure that John ever understood all the ceremonies and traditions of the faith. He often told me, using a baseball metaphor, that he believed and loved being a Catholic, but that he rode the pine like a second-string player.

Chapter 14:
1973 – Undercover at Lake Naivasha Lodge

Our old Volkswagen bus continued to give us trouble from time to time. In early February, after sharing a social evening with Howard and Anita at their home, Howard handed us an envelope filled with money and had us sign a paper for it, using our code names, Betsy and Babe.

John asked, 'What's this for, Howard?'

'To be able to do the work we have planned for you, you'll need a more reliable car. I want you to put this money toward the purchase of a late model used car. You may have to supplement it with your own money, but this will help. You'll get a little money with a trade on the bus, but for *God's sake* find a decent vehicle that doesn't break down every month!'

We smiled sheepishly at Howard. Once again, he was making our lives a little easier. I wondered if Howard's son Chris, who was playing rugby for Harlequins, had mentioned that several weeks before our bus had stalled while driving back from an away game in Kitale. The old green bus gave out coming up the escarpment near the little Italian chapel. We stood with the girls by the side of the road for fifteen minutes wondering what to do. Luckily, other rugby players drove by and offered us a lift. We locked up the bus and gratefully hitched a ride home. The unusual thing was that when John went back for it the next morning in a tow truck, it was just as we had left it. Nothing had been taken. Maybe it was too old to be of value to anyone.

We were grateful to get a better car and say goodbye to the Volkswagen, which we traded in at the dealership. We had been putting a little money away each month, which helped purchase a late model greenish-gold Toyota station wagon and left the temperamental old bus on the car lot. Once again, Howard had miraculously made another headache go away for us. If our friends or colleagues wondered how our station in life seemed to be improving, they never said a word to us.

A few weeks later, our case manager, Fred, met us near the entrance of the New Stanley Hotel for a midmorning cup of coffee on an outside patio called the Thorn Tree Cafe. The New Stanley Hotel was a favorite haunt for locals and tourists as a place to meet and gossip. It was fun to watch shoppers popping in and out of stores and local vendors selling trinkets to tourists along the boulevard.

Opening in 1902, as the Victoria Hotel, the hotel became the oldest hotel in Kenya. Originally built by Mayence Bent, the name soon changed to the Stanley Hotel and became a popular stopping point for people traveling by rail or going on safari. Bent renamed the hotel after Sir Morton Stanley, a Welsh explorer who famously found missionary and explorer, David Livingston, who had lost contact with the outside world for six years. In 1913 a new 60-room hotel was built on Delamere Avenue. A plan was made to transfer the Stanley Hotel to the new site with that name, but a legal battle ensued. Afterward, the old hotel became known as the Old Stanley with the new location adopting the name the New Stanley Hotel. In 1922, the hotel became the first place to sell Kenya's Tusker Beer beginning with a modest first shipment of ten bottles. 1932 marked the opening of the New Stanley Long Bar, which today is known as the Exchange Bar. Most of the structure was torn down and rebuilt by Jewish entrepreneur Abraham Brock and family in 1958 on the corner of Kenyatta Avenue and Kimathi Street. The hotel has hosted world leaders, authors, and film actors, including Winston Churchill, Ernest Hemingway, and Clark Gable.

Whenever we met, Fred always appeared a little on edge. Over time, we had gotten accustomed to him darting his eyes back and forth taking in the scene around him. We ordered coffee and scones and waited for him to lower his voice so only we could hear.

'We have good intel that a Russian diplomat, working at their embassy, is having an affair. We believe he plans to take the woman to Lake Naivasha Lodge this weekend. We want you to make reservations for your family to spend the weekend there. A young couple with their two daughters will not draw any unwarranted suspicion. Take your camera and binoculars.

Observe what guests are there and where they might be from. If the opportunity presents itself, engage the couple in innocent conversation. A surreptitious photo would be extremely useful.'

Moving his head to see if anyone was watching, Fred casually unfolded a *Daily Nation* newspaper that had been resting on the table. We looked down and could see that an envelope had been placed inside it. 'This money should cover the cost of the expenses for the weekend but keep your receipts and we will make adjustments as necessary.'

Fred had John *sign* the envelope, using his code name, Babe, and he casually placed the receipt in the breast pocket of his sport coat. At the conclusion of our meeting, Fred paid the coffee bill, said goodbye, and left without taking the newspaper with him. We waited another five minutes before leaving. John gathered the newspaper under his arm to take along with us.

We booked a room for the weekend at the lodge, packed our suitcases, and drove the girls in our newly acquired Toyota station wagon down the Rift Valley escarpment to Lake Naivasha. We were excited to visit a place that would not have normally been within our budget as teachers at NIS.

* * * * * *

Lake Naivasha Country Club opened in 1937 in the British Colonial Style and was popular with early expatriates. It was first known as the Lake Hotel in the 1930s before its renovation and becoming a stylish country club. Rooms and cottages were available for residents and guests. Comfortable Adirondack chairs and benches dotted the vast green lawns, which were shaded with mature acacia trees, providing outside relaxation. The Residents Lounge contained a massive fireplace and large bay windows, with comfortable couches and chairs for guests to read or visit. The dinner bill of fare was set each day and served with several courses and a dessert. Guests were then directed to the lounge area for coffee, brandy, or port while enjoying the fireplace. Near the lounge, a long bar with polished wood bordered a billiards room, which contained both billiard and snooker tables in the British tradition for guests who preferred a bit of movement after dinner. Other guests could enjoy card games or other activities like chess or backgammon.

We checked into our room on Friday afternoon and decided to take a tour of the property. John carried our camera and binoculars along with us as typical tourists might do. The girls ran ahead on the large expanse of grass, chasing a variety of exotic birds that were fed and inhabited the hotel. East African Crown Crested Cranes and Secretary Birds mingled with other bird species on the grass. We strolled along looking and listening for someone who looked or spoke Russian. We had no photo of what our target looked like. From time to time, we stopped and had friendly chats with other guests who, like us, were enjoying a stroll on the property or sitting in an Adirondack chair under the shade of an acacia tree.

Fred had given us a brief summary and loose description of the Russian they suspected would be a guest at the lodge that weekend, but after our tour of the property, we encountered no one fitting that description.

'Maybe we'll have better luck at dinner tonight,' John said.

The lodge served a set dinner and the bill of fare for the evening included roasted lamb with mint sauce, roasted potatoes, carrots, and spring peas, with peach melba for dessert. The food and service were wonderful, but we were focused on completing the task we had been assigned. Neither of us were able to relax and enjoy the moment, which at any other time would have been charming. After dinner, we were escorted to the comfortable lounge for coffee and after-dinner drinks in soft leather chairs. I could tell that Shauna and Tara were getting tired.

'I think I'll take the girls to our room and call it a night.'

John agreed and walked us back to our room. When the girls were settled into bed, John said, 'I'll head back to the lounge area and try to engage the guests in conversation. Maybe I can encourage some to join me in playing a little pool. I'll offer to buy a few glasses of Cognac and see what the guests can share with me.' John had honed his pool-playing skills during his college years at *The Billiard Den* on El Cajon Boulevard. He was good at it.

'Try not to win!' I cautioned. John laughed and took the key to our room and closed our door, locking it from outside.

I looked at the girls who were sharing a bed across the room. They were almost asleep. Sleep evaded me and I filled the time reading. Around eleven John returned. I could tell by the look on his face that he had come up short in finding information on the Russian and his girlfriend.

'I asked all sorts of questions, without making anyone suspicious, but there seemed to be no one around with a Russian accent.'

We ended up spending the entire weekend searching for the Russian man and his mistress to no avail. A part of us sensed we had let the team down. We felt a little guilty that we had been given this lovely weekend holiday but could not complete the mission. In truth, we never really felt relaxed enough to actually enjoy the moment.

We rarely ever discussed business with Fred over the phone. He preferred to meet us at his house or in the park or at a café. Sometimes he would show up at a rugby game and casually sit next to me in the stands, which he did the following Saturday. I greeted him casually, and we talked about how John and the team were doing. At some point, when I felt no one was paying attention to us, I lowered my voice to a whisper and expressed our sadness at the failure to complete the mission; he waved it off with his hand.

Leaning in and lowering his voice he said, 'Some of the tips we receive turn out to be false leads. It's just the way it is. It's not your fault, and I hope you enjoyed your weekend.'

'The hidden agenda made our time at the lodge not as relaxing as we had hoped.'

We later learned from Howard that many of the Russians who worked for their state department could not afford to stay at the lodge but used a less expensive camping site somewhere else near the lake.

Chapter 15:
Rob and Sue Evans

Among the many acquaintances and friends, we made, John and I had become very close with an English couple named Rob and Sue Evans. They had two daughters, Lonny and Blythe, who were close in age to our girls, and we enjoyed spending time with them. The Evans were non-playing members of Harlequin Rugby Club. Rob had a lucrative job working for a company named Chubb, which supplied businesses and hotels in Nairobi with safes and security devices.

Rob and Sue were a strikingly handsome young couple. In London, Rob had worked as a print and television model and had been quite the man about town with a large circle of friends. Rob had a passion for sailing and the sea. He once landed a television commercial for Cadbury's chocolate because the company needed a model who knew how to sail a small craft. Rob was a natural for the job, with his blond hair and strikingly handsome looks, to entice the public to buy their chocolate, as he sailed in the little boat they had rented for him.

Rob owned a sailboat and loved to go sailing with his friends in the ocean on the weekends. Often, he entered his boat in a regatta. He invited Sue on several of these outings. He instructed her to harness herself at the waist to a trapeze which was fixed to a wire attached to the mast and jump off the side of the boat with only her feet touching the edge. The purpose of this maneuver is to increase the speed of his vessel. Sue attached herself to the harness and prepared to click her harness onto the wire. In an unfortunate accident, Sue clipped her harness to the wire, but it didn't catch. She went flying overboard into the ice-cold water. Sailboats are difficult to reposition, so Rob finished the race before turning to retrieve her from the ocean. He apologized but told her the race must go on.

They dated for several years but Sue never knew if his affections were serious. As Sue told the story, he would call and invite her on outings with his friends, but at the end of their dates, he would drop her home and say goodnight without making future plans. His standard phrase was, 'I'll call you.'

Sue became increasingly worried that Rob never seemed to want to commit—even to secure a next date. Sue understood that part of Rob's reluctance to take the relationship further was their age difference. Rob was twelve years older than Sue and was often teased by his friends for *robbing the cradle*. Deep down, Sue understood that Rob was concerned with their difference in age and wanted Sue to date and have other experiences, but her heart was with Rob.

Sue felt the relationship was not moving in a forward direction. She decided to move to Australia at the request of an old beau. Sue's departure stunned Rob, forcing him to conclude that he was desperately in love with her and had been so for many years. Realizing he was in peril of losing her, Rob called her in Australia and begged her to return to England with a proper proposal of marriage. Within weeks, they were married and quickly moved to Nairobi for Rob's new business contract working for Chubb.

Rob was a great storyteller and would amuse us with his reflections of when he came to understand how close he came to losing Sue. His recounting of finally realizing how much he loved her was both endearing and hilarious. He talked of moping around London and driving his friends mad with his foolishness at not declaring himself to her sooner. We would roar with laughter as he told us of developing a facial tic when Sue moved to Australia and him thinking he had foolishly lost her forever. Like our friend, Norm Wiley, Rob was a master storyteller, using self-deprecating incidents to regale us in laughter.

Sue and I soon discovered that we shared a love of books, cooking and entertaining friends with dinner parties. She had a lovely voice and was a great sport, joining Jan Ellis and me the first time we sang at Harlequins. Although Rob was not a playing member of the rugby team, he and Sue were vital members of the club—supporting the team and participating in all the social activities. Sue and Rob shared a zest for life and harnessed their creative spirits in organizing several memorable dinner dances at the club. John and I were happy to lend a hand to ensure the success of each event. They spent weeks planning and organizing the decorating and dinner menu for their lavish events. They once turned the rugby club into a French bistro for *Bobbies Bistro Night,* complete with signs and umbrellas, to lend a French café look to the club.

To honor the 1974 film with Robert Redford, *The Great Gatsby*, they organized a dinner/dance by turning Harlequins into a Roaring Twenties style club, complete with a Twenties' dinner menu, period costumes, and music. Hosting these elaborate themed-based parties filled a creative spark which both Rob and Sue possessed, and we loved attending their parties.

Rob and Sue were also extremely generous friends. Rob would call John and say, 'Let's meet for dinner and dancing at the New Stanley Hotel.'

'Rob, we of course would love to, but you know Linda and I can't afford something like that on our teaching salary.'

'Never mind,' he would always retort, 'we'll put this one on the expense account with Chubb. These business dinners are an expected part of the job. Now we won't have another word on the subject.'

Weeks would go by, and Rob would call again and say, 'I hear there's a new chef at the Hilton Hotel and their Spaghetti Bolognese is first rate. We should go.'

Rob and Sue never took no for an answer, even though they knew we could never reciprocate in kind. We were so grateful and looked forward to getting dressed up and sharing delicious food. We loved their generous spirit.

Rob and Sue—vacationing in Mombasa

* * * * * *

John and I met Fred for one of our meetings at his house to sign papers using our code names. At the close of our meeting Fred said, 'The agency needs a large truck for an operation, and we don't want to use a vehicle from the agency. Howard wants to know if you might know someone who could loan us one for a night with no questions asked.'

John immediately thought of Rob. He knew Chubb had several large lorries, which they used to transport heavy safes and other office supplies to various businesses.

'I think I might know someone who would be able to help you out, Fred.'

'Yes, but would they be willing to do it with no questions asked?'

'I believe so. Let me get back to you.'

John approached Rob and said he needed to borrow a truck. 'I need a rather large lorry for an American friend of mine, but that's about all I can say.'

Rob never hesitated and offered, 'No worries, John. Just give me a few days' notice and I'll make one available for you.' He never questioned John further on the subject, which is what a true friend does when asked for a favor.

Fred was delighted and laid out the plans, which included the evening and time the vehicle would be called into service. 'Ask your friend if you might pick it up from his place of business in the evening and you will return it to him the following morning. On the appointed evening, Linda will follow you to a destination, which we will give to you later. You are to leave the truck with the keys hidden under the driver's seat. An agent will call you in the morning to retrieve the truck at the same place. This is terrific John. You've really helped us out.'

'Fred, I know our friend will not want anything in return for this favor, but Linda and I would like to take him and his wife out for a nice meal to say thanks. He and his wife have been very generous in treating us for a night out from time to time and we would love to return the favor. I believe this would be fair.'

'Let me run it by Howard, but I see no problem treating them to a meal on the agency.' Fred got back to us and told us to keep our receipts for the dinner and the agency would reimburse us for our evening out with Rob and Sue.

The operation with the truck went off according to plan. Of course, we never knew what it had been used for. We had learned early on that the CIA operated on a need-to-know basis to keep missions as tidy as possible. A few weeks later we met Rob and Sue to go to the movies.

There were several really nice movie theaters in Nairobi, which we took advantage of whenever a new movie came to town. Most of our friends did not have televisions and the programs that were available were limited. A night out at a cinema was an enjoyable event. Nairobi had strict rules regarding explicit sex and violence and often the shows had been edited to meet the standards set forth by the government.

The thing we loved most about the movie theaters was that we could book the tickets ahead and the seats could be reserved. We often met our friends early for a drink in the upstairs lounge. It was relaxing and when a bell was rung to indicate the start of the movie, we knew our reserved seats would be waiting for us.

As we sat in the lounge, John sipped on his drink and addressed our friends. 'Rob and Sue, Linda and I are so grateful for the loan of Chubb's company lorry, that we would like to treat you to a dinner show at the Intercontinental Hotel.'

Rob raised his hand in a gesture saying it was not necessary. I interrupted and added, 'It will be our treat to say thanks for not only loaning us the company truck, but…well, all the many times you have treated us, as you love to say, *on the company.*'

'Are you certain? You know that it's not necessary and the Intercontinental can be a bit pricey. Why don't we just go Dutch,' offered Rob.

'Not this time, Rob,' answered John.

'I hear that there is a new singer there who's had wonderful reviews,' added Sue. In the end, they accepted our invitation with no more objections.

We made reservations for a Saturday night and donned our best outfits for a fancy evening and a dinner show. Many of the restaurant hotels in Nairobi were designed in the style of the thirties and reminded me of those old Fred Astaire movies. Patrons were seated at tables that bordered a large dance floor. The evening meal was designed to flow at a leisurely pace. Drinks and food would be ordered upon being seated, and it was common for guests to get up and have a whirl around the dance floor in between courses to the music of a full orchestra. The restaurant expected that most of their guests would be enjoying the dinner and entertainment for most of the night. I often thought it was a very civilized way to have a meal and a far cry from anything I had ever experienced in California.

The singer who headlined the event took to the stage as we were enjoying our main course. It was the first time I had ever ordered Steak Diane and was delighted when the chef came to our table to grill the steak and finish it in a flourish of flaming brandy. We enjoyed the featured singer as we ate the lovely entrees. For John and me, it was a treat to enjoy the evening with no thought of the cost. We were secretly delighted that we could finally treat our dear friends after being on the receiving end of so many memorable meals courtesy of them.

Later that evening, I remember being a little sheepish when John showed me the bill. 'That was the most expensive meal we've ever paid for. I hope Howard agrees.'

John said, 'I think it's fair, Linda. I imagine it would have been pretty costly to rent a large truck.' He later said that Howard was very gracious when John presented him with the receipt.

Chapter 16:
Summer 1973 – No-speak-a-da Dutch

Often John and I would whisper quietly in bed at night and then burst into giggles at the things we were doing for the agency. It may have been the recklessness of our youth, but we were never worried about the dangerous aspects of the job, although in retrospect, I'm certain there were times when we should have been. Mostly, we were amazed at our good fortune. The quality of our lives *had* greatly improved since being recruited to work for the CIA. We had better housing, a better car, and were comforted that money was being put into our banking account in San Diego. We continued taping our neighbors whenever they had guests over for a party. We handed the tapes off to Fred, never knowing what information they may have contained. Fred told us the tapes were sent off to Washington DC for evaluation. We continued to nurture our relationships with our Middle Eastern neighbors, Mohammed and Babekka, and the suspected Russian KGB operative, Sergei.

We had completed our two-year contract with Nairobi International School and were eager to sign a new contract to extend our employment with NIS for another two years. As part of our initial contract with USIU, we were scheduled to go on home leave for the summer of 1973. United States International University would cover the cost of the roundtrip flight for our family.

Shauna was almost five and Tara had just celebrated her third birthday. We decided to stop in Europe and visit Belgium, Austria, and Germany for the first week of our trip home to California. Our Sabina Airline plane landed in Vienna. We hustled the girls through the airport to retrieve our luggage and follow the maze of directions to the car rental area. John and I were completely absorbed in following the signs and arrows in the terminal. Both of the girls had been unusually quiet, but we just assumed they were tired from the flight.

From time to time, Shauna had been pulling on John's jacket and calling out his name.

'Daddy, daddy.'

To which he would reply, 'In a minute, Shauna. Daddy is a little busy right now.'

'But Daddy.'

This exchange went on for several minutes.

Finally, out of breath and slightly flustered, John looked down at his five-year-old-daughter and asked in exasperation, 'What is it, Shauna? Daddy's a little busy at the moment.'

He looked down to see a little girl with eyes as wide as saucers and his eyes softened. 'What is it, honey. You look like you've seen a ghost.'

Shauna pointed back at the airport terminal and said, 'Daddy. This is a magic house!'

John and I looked at each other and wondered why she would feel this way, until it quickly dawned on us. Living in Kenya, the girls had never been exposed to a modern airport. In the space of an hour, we had passed through countless automatic doors, ridden up and down several escalators, and dragged our luggage over moveable walkways. Things that we naturally took for granted were all new to our little Kenya girls.

John picked her up and gave her a gentle squeeze. 'Yes, honey, I can see why you might think that. On this trip you're going to experience lots of new things that you have never seen before. Wait until we visit Disneyland with your cousins, Chad and Julia. You're going to have so much fun.'

We enjoyed touring the city of Vienna for two nights before heading to the countryside. It was there that we learned a valuable lesson about taking photos. When we had the slides developed in San Diego for a showing, our family kept asking us: What is the name of this statue? Where did you see the fountain? Who is that guy on the horse? We could not remember the details of any of these photos and realized they were not interesting. In the future, we decided to focus on taking photos of family and the people we met on our journeys.

John packed our suitcases in a little red Opel rental car, and we tried to maneuver our way out of the city in the early morning. We hadn't gone two miles, when a loud siren blared at us from behind. We were surprised to see two policemen in a small Volkswagen beetle frantically motioning for us to pull to the side of the street. Our first thought amused us with the idea that policemen would be driving such a little car. We were used to seeing cops in much larger American made vehicles in California. We knew we must have done something fairly egregious because the officer who approached our car was furious.

Unfortunately, we didn't understand a word he was saying. The second policeman approached and began gesticulating, intimidating, and yelling at us in German. The policeman motioned for John to step out of our car.

John turned to me and asked, 'What shall I do? I don't know what we did wrong.'

I whispered to John 'Tell him we don't speak German.'

'What should I say?'

I had learned one German phrase from my friend Sylke Schimdt who with her husband Rolf, were nonplaying members of Harlequins.

'Politely say: *No spreche kein Deutsch.*' John turned to me with a look of horror in his eyes and tried to mouth the words.

The officers were getting annoyed with us. John exited the car to an onslaught of German words still being hurled at him by the officers as they waved their arms while pointing at the road to our rear.

John shook his head and looked at the officers in utter bafflement. After more screaming from the policemen, John threw his arms up and blurted out, '*No speak-a da Dutch*'.

I almost wet my pants trying not to laugh. Whatever the policeman said, John continued to look confused and continued repeating, '*No speak-a da Dutch*'. The officer motioned that he wanted identification and John showed him his Kenyan driver's license and his US passport, all the while repeating the phrase, *No speak-a da Dutch.*

Finally, in a last exasperated motion, the officer handed John back his documents, threw up his hands and pointed to the road that would take us out of his city. John put the car into first gear and slowly inched his way toward the road that would take us into the countryside.

'What did daddy do, Mommy?' asked Shauna. 'Those men were really mad.'

'I guess we made some sort of driving mistake, but daddy handled the situation perfectly with the nice police officers.'

'They didn't seem very nice,' offered Shauna.

'They were mean,' added Tara.

We were happy to reach the outside of the city and pull onto a country road. But every time we thought of it, we got the giggles.

'What did you want me to say?' asked John. 'I don't speak German.'

'Actually, you did simply fine. I don't know if the officers were frustrated over our breaking the law or your butchering of the German language. Actually, you were better than fine. It got us out of having to pay a fine or being hauled off to a police station.'

More laughter ensued from inside the little red Opel.

We did not have experience traveling internationally with two young girls, and the week in Europe was not as exciting as we had planned. Tara, at three, was bored touring the countryside in our little red Opal and kept asking, 'Daddy, when are we going to get there?'

Despite the constant chorus of, *'When are we going to get there?'* from Tara and trying to produce ways to keep the girls happy, we did manage to see gorgeous sections of Austria and Germany.

We drove into a delightful village in the Austrian alps and booked a night in a charming hotel, which had once been a convent for nuns. The building was like something out of a fairy tale, with window boxes filled with colorful flowers and trailing vines. We settled into our room and decided to take the girls for a stroll around the village for a sausage roll and an ice cream.

'I can't believe how quaint and clean everything is here, John.'

'I know. Everyone seems so industrious.' As we passed several A-frame houses with colorful window boxes filled with flowers, we saw villagers enjoying the day. The entire village was experiencing the warmth of a pleasant afternoon. Women were sweeping their front porches as men mowed their lawns or trimmed hedges. We walked past a small, forested area filled with pine trees and shrubs.

'Look, Mommy! A baby deer is eating leaves off that bush,' said Shauna.

To our delight, a small deer was indeed foraging for food nearby.

'I want to pet her,' whispered Tara.

'We don't want to frighten the little deer,' counseled John. 'Let's walk very slowly and we'll see how close it will let us get to it.'

The girls were excited as they moved timidly toward the animal, inching ever closer so as to not spook it into running away. We had gotten within five yards of the little deer, who still seemed unperturbed by our advancements. John held out his hand indicating that we should stop. We stood looking in amazement as the delicate little fawn continued munching on the leaves of a bush. We looked on for several minutes, hardly taking a breath.

All of a sudden, we heard a voice in the distance calling for what we assumed was their child or a dog. 'Frisky... Frisky...Frisky. *Komm her*, Frisky.'

The small deer lifted its head and turned in the direction of the noise. A second later it scampered in the direction of the sound. We looked on in amazement as a woman, standing near her front door, reached down and petted the head of her dear little deer, AKA...Frisky.

'Oh, my goodness! No wonder the little dear let us get so close to it. Frisky is not a wild deer, but someone's pet,' I chuckled.

'I want a deer for a pet,' voiced Shauna.

'I want one too,' chimed Tara.

'Well, right now let's get you girls something to eat for dinner in town and, if you're good, an ice cream,' offered John.

'Then a bath and you're off to bed,' I instructed.

We bathed and tucked the girls in bed together and I told them a bedtime story. Soon they drifted off to sleep in a queen-size bed under a beautiful white down duvet. It was the first one I had ever seen, as there was nothing like it in California at the time. When it seemed, they were down for the count, we slipped out of the room and headed downstairs for a pleasant meal and bottle of wine at the hotel dining room.

Looking back on it, we realized it was foolish to leave the girls unattended in our room, but we were young and fortunately, we found them sound asleep when we returned.

Later, I grieved for the parents who left their kidnapped three-year-old daughter unattended in their hotel room, while they ate a meal with friends in Portugal. The incident brought chills as to what might have happened to us in a foreign country.

John and I loved seeing this part of Europe for the first time, but it was not as exciting for Tara, who kept asking as we drove through sites like the Black Forest, 'Daddy, when are we going to get there?'

Eventually, we did *get there* and arrived in San Diego for a four-week stay with our families. The girls had never met their cousins, Chad and Julia, but as kids do, they became fast friends within the span of an hour. We spent time at the beach, where John was invited by his high school friend, Ron Fox, to play in the 1973 *Over the Line Tournament*. We visited the world-famous San Diego Zoo, where my sister Diane, who worked in the *Children's Zoo,* gave us a VIP tour of the enclosure. Through Aunt Diane, the cousins were able to get special treatment and enjoyed petting and feeding *Champ*, a baby elephant, and *Binder,* a baby rhinoceros. The cousins also delighted in visiting Disneyland and Knotts Berry Farm.

**John playing in the *Over the Line Tournament* with Linda
watching in the two-piece bathing suit
I had made in Nairobi**

The Over the Line Tournament began in San Diego and consists of three-person teams played at the beach in the sand. Sponsored by (OMBAC) the Old Mission Beach Athletic Club, the tournament is celebrating its seventy-first year of play in 2024.

Chapter 17:
A Fight, a Flight, and a Family Surprise

After visiting with the family for a month, we boarded a plane in San Diego to fly to England via Colorado and New York. We wanted to squeeze every moment of fun out of our visit, so we grabbed a flight to Denver, Colorado, to visit friends.

John had been given a beautiful set of golf clubs from Louisville Slugger when he had signed to play for the Los Angeles Dodgers organization and wanted to bring them back to Kenya. There was no issue with the extra weight of the clubs at the airport in San Diego.

We were met at the airport by Doc and Josie Gilbert and driven to Arvada, Colorado, to spend a few days at their home. The Gilberts were the same family we had toured with to Lake Turkana when John was baptized. It was a great visit, after which, they took us to the airport for our next flight to New York, where we would catch a connecting flight to London.

At the Denver airport we encountered a young man who was giving us a tough time about the extra weight of the golf clubs. John explained that we had no trouble with the clubs in San Diego. The attendant would not budge on the issue and argued with us until we missed our flight to New York. We couldn't believe we were stuck in Denver without a flight. We were frantic and I knew this would mean we would not arrive in London at our scheduled time and before the age of cell phones, it would be difficult to alert Rob Evans who was picking us up at Heathrow Airport. John was furious. He loaded our luggage on a cart and went over to the counter of Continental Airlines, with the girls and me trailing behind like lost puppies.

John explained our predicament to the attendant. A sweet young agent looked at our two girls and their mother who was visibly distraught. She checked her register and smiled. 'I have four seats on a flight to New York leaving in one hour. There are only first-class seats available, but I can see you are in a bit of a bind. I will book you at the same price you paid the other airline.' She never gave any thought to the golf clubs and merely loaded everything onto the conveyor belt for boarding.

She was so compassionate. To this day, I am grateful for her kindness to our family. Flying by today's standards is not fun. Passengers are herded on the plane and pointed in the direction of a narrow seat with little leg room, minimal comfort, and even fewer amenities.

I will never forget flying first class with Continental in the summer of 1973. An airline hostess seated us at a low table with two seats on each side facing one another just like we were in a restaurant. John sat with Shauna, and I sat with Tara. Neither of us knew what to expect. A few minutes later, a stewardess, who looked pretty enough to be a model, approached and asked if we would like a complimentary glass of champagne or a cocktail. John and I looked at each other, not certain what to say. It had been a stressful morning, and a drink sounded really nice.

'Thank you, miss, but to be honest we don't even belong here. We missed our flight, and a kind agent gave us these seats. We didn't pay for them,' I sheepishly offered.

This beautiful angel smiled and said, 'Well, whether or not you paid full price for your seats, *anyone* who sits in this section of the plane is entitled to all the amenities offered in first-class. There is no extra charge.'

John and I looked at each other and relaxed for the first time that day. 'Yes, we would love a glass of champagne,' said John.

'Good, and I'll bring the girls a Shirley Temple, with your permission of course.'

'They would love that.'

We sipped our drinks and waited for the plane to take off. After an hour, our angel came by with a trolley carrying four trays of gorgeous food with silverware, beautiful cloth napkins, and crystal-stemmed glasses. The delicious meal of steak, potatoes, and a spinach souffle was served on fine China plates accompanied with a wine of our choosing. I felt as though we were dining in a fancy five-star restaurant. I thought nothing else could surprise me on that flight, but after our meal our attendant pushed a cart in front of us with an array of cakes, pastries, and fruit. Towering in the middle of the trolley stood a cone-shaped mountain of frozen ice cream balls at least a foot high and in every flavor and color one could imagine. Shauna and Tara stared with delight as they chose their respective flavors, which were carefully removed from the display and placed in crystal bowls.

I often think about that flight when I'm herded on a plane like cattle and offered few amenities and service. It was magical. I wrote to the company and thanked them for assisting us when we were in need. I always made it a practice to fly Continental if I could. Continental Airlines went out of business in 2012 when they merged with United Airlines.

By the time we reached New York, the girls were cranky and tired. The unique magic of the airport terminal had vanished. Their Grandma Sue had given them each a doll and a doll case at the San Diego airport. John and I were already burdened with masses of luggage and told the girls they would have to be responsible for these gifts. As we made our way to our connecting flight from New York to London, three-year-old Tara dropped her doll and case on the floor. No amount of coaxing could get her to go back and pick them up. I was prepared to leave them when five-year-old Shauna ran back and gathered the items in her arms, along with her own doll and case. It was an extremely sweet gesture by Tara's older sister. We encountered zero hassle with the airline about the golf clubs.

We had become quite close with Rob and Sue Evans, and they had invited us to visit them in England for a week at an investment property they owned. The house resided in an area called Burnam on Crouch, which they were preparing to sell. We fell in love with England's charming towns and beautiful countryside and our girls were happy to play with Lonny and Blythe. The Evans treated us to a beautiful pub lunch and an excursion at the Ferry Boat Inn. To this day, London and the countryside of England are among my favorite places to visit.

After a short flight to Brussels, we were maneuvering through the same *magical house* terminal from six weeks before to catch our last plane flight to Kenya. A businessman, who was not paying attention to where he was going, smacked right into Tara and knocked her back. Tara was in no mood for his carelessness. She put her hands on her hips and glared up at him. He blinked his eyes and took a step backwards when the young three-year-old barked, 'Watch where you're going, mister!'

At that moment I knew that no one would ever take advantage of that little lady. I also knew that her older sister would always have her back. Flying southward on our final flight to Kenya, Shauna looked at us and said, 'I don't like airplane food. It's boring!'

I turned to John and whispered, 'Ah, the discerning palate of a five-year-old, who has been tainted by the luxuries of first-class dining.'

The thrill of flying had come full circle.

* * * * * *

The six-week home visit had gone by in a flash, and we were ready to start a new year at NIS and to continue our work with the CIA.

Before the 1973 school term was ready to begin, John and I agreed to go on a camping trip to the Aberdare Mountains for a weekend with our friend, Norm Wiley, and his son, Mark. Aberdare Park was where our old green bus had broken down on our first camping trip with Chris Bane. We were delighted to camp in the same spot next to the trout stream.

During the past two years, we had purchased some camping equipment and were better prepared for the incredibly cold nights. We drove up on a Friday with a plan to stay two nights and come home on Sunday, just as we had done with Chris Bane.

On Saturday, Norm headed down the mountain to Nyeri to get gas and treat the kids to an ice cream. The day was sunny and warm, and John and I set out a blanket next to the trout stream. Little did we suspect that nine months later our family would increase with the addition of our beautiful son, Joshua Scott. Josh has always loved the outdoors and especially fishing. We told him it is probably because he was conceived beside a trout stream with elephants and other wild game in the distance.

Josh has always been enormously proud to have been born in Nairobi and have dual citizenship, so I will share two funny stories about him when he was a little boy. It can be cold in the winter in California, especially in Hemet where we lived when we came back from Africa. Once, on a particularly chilly day, Josh, age four, started to run out the front door of our house to play without shoes on.

I yelled, 'Joshua, come back this instant and put your shoes on. It's cold outside!'

To which he replied, looking back over his shoulder, and running like the gingerbread man, 'I don't have to, Mom. I'm

African!' He kept on running and I couldn't help but laugh as I watched him go.

Josh was a social little boy and would strike up conversations with strangers when we might be standing in a store ready to check out. Once, we were in line at a hardware store when Josh, who was about five at the time, struck up an exchange with a large man standing in front of us who was wearing western boots and a cowboy hat.

Josh tugged on his shirt and asked, 'Hey mister, are you a cowboy?'

The man turned and looked at Josh. He laughed and replied, 'No son. I'm not a cowboy, I'm an Indian.' (Hemet has many Indians who live on the Soboba Indian reservation).

Josh pondered this information and nodded. The tall Indian man eventually bent down and asked, 'Hey son, are you a cowboy?'

Josh thought for a minute and shook his head. 'No—I'm African.'

The kind man looked at me with a confused expression, until I explained that my son was born in Kenya and did indeed have dual citizenship.

Chapter 18:
Taping and a Tape Worm

We were delighted we were expecting a new addition to our family. Since living in Kenya, I had been very much into physical fitness—jogging, playing squash, and taking exercise classes while the girls were in school. I was in the initial stages of my pregnancy and planned to continue my daily workouts. I received the okay from Doctor Papworth who agreed that I was in excellent health, although my blood pressure was a little low.

Over the course of the next few weeks, I noticed that I would suddenly feel faint. John noted that my blood pressure continued to be low. Whenever I became light in the head, I would bend over and thrust my head between my legs until the dizziness passed. After a jog at Nairobi College or finishing an exercise workout, I would often shop in the city. It became a frequent practice for me to be shopping in a store and out of the blue get lightheaded. The dropping of my head between my legs always seemed to cure the problem and soon the episode would pass, and I would continue what I was doing. I perceived it had something to do with being pregnant and exercising, but I was not overly concerned. I made a mental note to mention it to Doctor Papworth during my next visit.

John and I felt blessed to have servants help with the house and our children. George and the other servants were given Saturday afternoon and all-day Sunday off. John and I made it a fun practice to put the girls to bed after their dinner and enjoy a Sunday evening date night with just the two of us. Often, John would cook for me. He might grill something outside in the summer, or we might cook sausages or pork chops in our fireplace in the winter. One Sunday night, we decided to have a picnic-style meal with finger food on our bed.

I had just taken a hot bath, donned my nightgown, and sat up in bed to eat our repast with a glass of wine. I have never been a big drinker, but this was before the rules on abstaining from alcohol while pregnant. At some point, John noticed a flat white object that looked like a piece of fettuccine pasta, which was moving along the sheet. We stared at it thinking our eyes were playing tricks on us. Suddenly, I screamed in horror. It all came swimming into my brain. The lightheadedness, and the bending over until the blood rushed back into my head.

'That thing came out of me! What is it?'

John watched the *thing* for a few moments and said, 'Linda, I think you have a tape worm, and I believe your hot bath forced part of it to come out.'

I was in a sheer state of panic and wanted him to take me to the emergency room immediately. John, being the voice of reason, calmed me down.

'Linda, think about it. In all likelihood, you've had this living inside you for months. I think we should go to bed, and we'll deal with it first thing in the morning.'

The picnic and date night became the furthest thing from our minds.

The next day at the doctor's office, I informed Doctor Papworth of my lightheaded episodes, and he confirmed that I did indeed have a tape worm. The fainting spells were a result of the tapeworm robbing nutrients from my system. The doctor said he had seen it happen before.

'How did I get it?' I asked.

'Lots of times, to save money, uninspected meat is sold to a restaurant at the back door. If it isn't cooked properly, a person can become infected. Judging from your description of finding a part of the worm on the sheet, you have had this one for quite some time. I will write you a prescription that will kill it, and I will give you a purgative to expel it once it's dead.' He said there should be no problem with me being pregnant, but it was good that I had discovered it so early in my pregnancy.

'How long will it take to kill it and get it out of me?'

'Oh, it shouldn't take more than a day or two.'

A day or two never happened. I may have been overly anxious with the thought of a tapeworm living inside me, which may have made my system stall, but it took four uneasy days for the poison and purgative to do its job. In the end, an exceedingly long, bloated, and dead tapeworm was expelled from my body.

Reader, I'm sure as you visualize this mess in my toilet, I can imagine that you are filled with horror. I will tell you that you are not wrong. I may have flushed the beast from my bathroom commode, but I had trouble flushing it from my mind.

Two weeks later Anita Bane and I were invited to an English woman's home for one of our monthly group gourmet luncheons. The woman, whose husband worked for the British Consulate, treated us to a traditional roast beef and Yorkshire pudding dinner. She served chicken noodle soup for the first course. I stared at the soup but could not force myself to dip my spoon in the bowl. Anita noticed that I had turned pale and asked if I was okay. I nodded and was able to sip on the broth and eat a few carrots. In removing the soup bowl, our hostess noticed a pile of uneaten noodles. I told her it was lovely, but I wanted to save my appetite for the main course. In truth, I could not look at or eat pasta that even resembled fettuccine for years. I had PTSD over that nightmare for a long time.

* * * * * *

Preparing for the addition to our family brought us joy and a few concerns. The manufactured stone stairs to our duplex could be treacherous if one were to fall. They led up to a landing and turned in the opposite direction and led straight into our living room with no door separating the stairs from the living quarters. The duplex was fine for the girls, who understood they needed to be incredibly careful, but the duplex was not set up for a baby. The stairs could be fatal for a baby or young toddler if they were to fall. I mentioned this to Howard, and he gave me permission to begin looking for another house in our neighborhood.

I discovered that an American couple that worked for Firestone was leaving the country. I ran into the woman at the market, and she suggested we rent their three-bedroom bungalow, which was a block away from our duplex.

I explained the new living accommodations to Howard. He graciously agreed that it would be fine if the new property were close enough to get wireless reception.

'We have a device that can check for that. Is there any way you can assess it?'

'I don't think that would be a problem. The woman has students at NIS, and I can arrange to call on her to look over the property.'

This became wonderful news. If the radio frequency carried to the next street over, it would allow us to continue our bugging operation. Plus, we would be in a safer house for the new baby. Howard notified Fred and we set up a meeting at his home. Fred gave me a device that would measure radio frequency to see if it would reach the new distance.

A few days later, I visited the woman who lived in the bungalow. She was incredibly accommodating when I explained my purpose was to check out the property before moving there. After sharing a coffee and a tour of the house, I asked if I could use the bathroom facilities. I went in and removed the device from my large handbag. The box had a needle pointing upward toward the colors of red, yellow, and green. If the needle pointed to green, it would verify there was enough radio frequency power to reach the targeted houses.

My hands were shaking as I turned the dial to the correct frequency. To my delight, the device's arrow moved to the green area. I breathed a sigh of relief that there was indeed enough power to continue our bugging operation of the Russian, Sergei, and our duplex neighbors, Mohammed and Babekka. I was thrilled.

Chapter 19:
1974 – A New Home and A New Baby

There was one other huge hurdle with renting the new house and once again Howard came to our rescue. Other than a stove and refrigerator, the bungalow did not come furnished. Over the past two years, we had purchased or acquired beds and other small pieces of furniture from expats who had left Kenya. We were missing a dining table and chairs, a dining room sideboard for dishes, a couch, and armchairs for the lounge area. Howard graciously gave me a stipend with which to furnish what we needed. We were overcome with gratitude.

'Howard, this is too much.'

He waved me off. 'Not to worry. We often furnish the places where we house our assets. And whenever you leave Kenya, the furniture will remain the property of the government, which will be used in the future.' He set the amount he felt we would need to get the furniture we needed, and I set about shopping. It was so much fun!

I have always loved to decorate, but as a newly married couple on a budget in San Diego, the majority of our furniture came via secondhand or gifts from our parents. I now had the opportunity to pick out new furniture in the style and colors of my choice. I couldn't wait to visit the shops and see what I could afford on my budget. I enlisted the help of my friend, Sue Evans. We spent several mornings scouring shops in Nairobi looking for the things I needed.

The city of Nairobi was often congested with a lot of foot traffic. I had learned to guard my handbag close to my side. I had been warned of very skillful pickpockets who roamed the sidewalks looking for an unsuspecting tourist. As careful as I was, early in my time in Nairobi, I had my wallet picked from my handbag on an outing to an animal rescue park.

After a morning of shopping for prospective furniture, Sue and I decided to pop into Bobby's Bistro for a coffee and sandwich. As we made our way to the cafe, we witnessed a disturbance about twenty yards up the street. To me, it looked like an East Indian man had collapsed by the curb, and three Kenyan men were helping him into the back of an automobile. I walked toward the activity thinking I might be able to help.

As I moved closer to the scene, I heard Sue calling my name. 'Linda! Linda! You must stop. Come back here immediately!'

I turned around and saw my frantic friend motioning for me to follow her as she ducked inside a jewelry shop. It suddenly occurred to me that things were not exactly as I first thought. The man I believed to be in a distress was thrashing about as he was being thrust into the back of a car with all of its doors open. I then noticed other pedestrians scattering away from the scene. My head began to pound, and my heart started racing. It was all happening so fast. I quickly turned and retraced my steps to Sue. I entered the shop to see Sue, along with other people, huddled together looking out the window. The men had successfully stuffed the poor man into the back of their car. We stared at the scene until the vehicle made a screeching sound with its tires, as it sped down the street. My hands began to shake.

'My God, Linda, you almost got yourself killed!'

'I thought the man needed medical attention and wanted to help. What just happened?' I was annoyed with myself and reflected; *This is embarrassing for someone working undercover for the CIA. I should have been more on top of my game!*

The owner of the shop addressed the group. 'Well, the East Indian man was carrying a satchel, filled with yesterday's cash receipts and cheques from his shop to the bank. Those men were robbers and, in all likelihood, had been watching his movements for several weeks.'

I gasped and said, 'Oh, my Lord. They're going to kill him.'

'The penalty for murder is death in Kenya, and the prisons are brutal. They might just dump him somewhere once they separate him from his satchel.'

Within minutes, the activity on the street seemed to return to normal. A police car rolled up and we saw eyewitnesses gesticulating and sharing what they had seen. After we both had calmed down a bit, Sue and I walked to Bobby's Bistro, drank coffee, and relived the harrowing incident for the next half hour.

After a week of shopping, I decided on a couch and matching armchair that possessed a green and blue stripe on a thickly woven fabric. In another shop, I purchased a beautiful rocking chair, which would come in handy with the birth of our baby. The rocking chair was fitted with a rust-colored cushion and back rest. A mahogany dining room table with six chairs and matching sideboard completed what we needed for the bungalow.

John got to work and made us a beautiful coffee table and side tables out of thick wood. He was proud that he had used only wooden dowels and glue in putting the tables together. It looked perfect for our needs. He sanded it and stained the wood in a lovely walnut tone.

The lounge area had a long expanse of windows that looked out onto a small patio, which led to a large enclosed grassy area. I needed curtains to cover the windows in the lounge. To save money, I bought a huge bolt of beige burlap material and fashioned the curtains from that. We were thrilled that the girls could share a room, and the third bedroom would become a nursery for the new baby. Friends gifted us a crib and diaper changing table for the nursery.

I loved our new home and was happier than I had been since moving to Kenya. My life felt complete. I was thrilled living in a house, in a quiet neighborhood, with a beautiful back garden for the girls to play in. All was going well—until it wasn't.

The listening device was dismantled at the duplex and technicians came to set up the new operation. To my embarrassment, the technicians revealed that the new house was out of range and the wireless frequency did not work. I was devastated and assured our handler, Fred, that it had absolutely worked when I had evaluated it in the bathroom several months before. I was worried the agency might think I had lied about the range in order to move to a safer house for the new baby. Again, I felt we had let the team down.

If Fred was upset with us, he never let it show. 'I am positive that when you assessed the device it was working as you said. These things happen.'

Fred said we would continue to gather intel from the post-office boxes and do the odd assignment when called upon. We were also told that our house would be used as a *safe house*.

John asked, 'What will that entail for us?'

'You will have to vacate the house from time to time when our agents need to meet at a secret location to discuss various things.'

Fred would call and using a coded message would let us know that a meeting would be taking place at our home, and we would have to vacate the premises for X number of hours. This became a bit challenging with two young girls and a baby. Living in Nairobi in the seventies did not lend itself to being out in the evening. There were no indoor malls or fast-food restaurants. Other than eating at a curry restaurant or going to the movies, there was little to do at night with young children. Sometimes, we would pop in on our friend Norm, who had recently moved into the city and was living much closer to us.

Most of the time, we were given advance notice when these meetings were to take place. But sometimes we were blindsided and had to hurriedly pack up the car and were told to stay away from our house for X number of hours. One night we arrived home after vacating the house, and I answered a call from Fred who arranged a meeting for the next day.

'John, I have a feeling something went wrong. Fred sounded a little out of sorts.'

'We'll find out tomorrow.'

The next morning, we met Fred at The New Stanley Hotel for coffee at the outdoor Thorn Tree Café. 'Did everything go well at the safe house meeting last night?' asked John.

Fred looked unnerved and got straight to the point. 'Just so you know, two agents were sitting at your dining room table when a friend of yours named Norm Wiley knocked once and entered the house through the kitchen door. Your friend was surprised to see two strange men sitting at your dining room table. He asked where you were. The agents became a bit unnerved, trying to explain that you had gone out for a moment. Norm backed out the kitchen door and left. You'd better produce a relevant story as to who they were and why they were there.'

John told Norm he had been meeting two coaches from local schools to schedule a basketball tournament, when we rushed Tara to the emergency room with a fever. I'm not sure Norm ever believed the story, but we didn't offer anything further on the subject.

While working undercover we were often on edge. We didn't like deceiving our family and friends with false narratives when certain incidents arose. It grew to be more of an issue when we were told to vacate the house for clandestine meetings, which sometimes occurred on short notice. The tides were shifting, and we would soon have to make a crucial decision as to our future with the CIA.

**Front view of our third house with Tara and my little
Fiat, where I was so happy—1974**

Tara in the back garden of our beautiful bungalow and CIA safe house. Tara was going through her curtsying period for photos at this time.

* * * * * *

After returning from home leave in San Diego in 1973, Howard and Anita announced they were being assigned to work at The Hague in the Netherlands and would be leaving Nairobi the following summer.

Howard met with us to talk about going full time with the CIA. 'John would be the agent under contract. Linda, you would go in the capacity of his wife but of course would be a support asset behind the scenes. If you agree to proceed, I will arrange for John to have meetings with agents from Washington, take a few character tests, and undergo a polygraph test. I believe you both would serve your country with distinction, and I would be there as support if you choose to join the agency.'

We spent many nights talking about the pros and cons of going permanently with the agency. I knew that John was keener on the idea than I was.

'Why are you reluctant to make this move with the agency,' John asked as we had just gotten into bed one night. 'I'm sure the salary would be better than teaching. We've enjoyed working undercover, right?'

'Yes, Howard and the other agents have been great. If we decide to do this and you are accepted into the program, we have to be prepared that our family will be living the majority of our lives outside of the United States.'

'Are you afraid you'll miss your family in California, Linda?'

'Well, that may be part of it, but you must realize, John, that we will be at the bottom of the pecking order when it comes to assignments. We won't be posted to a lovely place like Kenya or The Hague. In all likelihood, we will be posted in Bangladesh or Pakistan. But even more than that, you are an amazing teacher and coach. All of your college training has led you to teaching and coaching. You have a gift. You truly touch the lives of your students.'

'I love being a teacher, Linda, but we would see so much of the world!'

'We would, but I've witnessed drinking within the organization. I mean, it would be so easy to fall into that trap with the price of a bottle of liquor being only two dollars. We would be expected to entertain and make contacts. I wonder what type of life it would be for our kids being posted to various places every few years. It could be an amazing experience, or they might resent not ever getting to know their cousins, aunts and uncles, or grandparents.'

We continued to talk about the pros and cons for the next two weeks, and Howard graciously let us take our time. It was an agonizing decision. In the end, John and I eventually decided to stay in the field of teaching and not pursue a career with the CIA. We didn't know it at the time, but it may have been the right choice.

> *In 1975 Congress commissions the Church Committee and the Pike Committee to investigate possible illegal activities by the CIA. The reports conclude that checks and balances need to be instituted and applied to preserve the constitutional rights of its citizens. The resulting findings lead to a restructuring of the CIA by tightening its numbers and operations over the next several years. The CIA's ordeals during the mid to late seventies may have made our decision to stay teaching the correct course.*

We were incredibly sad when the time came for the Banes to leave Kenya. They departed in June of 1974 along with their younger children, Peter, Janita, and Bethany. Just before leaving, Howard and Anita asked if their son, Christopher, could stay with us until the beginning of August when he would eventually journey to the Netherlands in route to Indiana University. We had loved Chris from that first camping safari to the Aberdare Mountains and were happy to have him as a guest in our home.

Barbara Schlesinger, a student from NIS, invited John and me to join her at the home of Michaela Denis to attend a séance. Michaela and her late husband Armand had made a series of wildlife television documentaries. They were regular fixtures on the BBC and ITV in the fifties and sixties. The couple eventually settled in Nairobi, Kenya. Armand died in 1971 of Parkinsons disease. and acting as medium during the séances, Michaela would take on the voices and personalities of various dead people.

Perhaps it was because Michaela lost Armand or perhaps it was a gift she had always possessed, but Michaela was convinced that she could commune with spirits. She would invite interested parties to her home to be escorted to a darkened room upstairs where she would bring forth various spirits through a voice that would often change with each ghostly appearance. I never experienced a paranormal incident, but John was thinking of his deceased father when he felt someone patting his shoulder. The odd thing was that there was no one sitting behind us. I stayed neutral on the séance, although John was forever convinced his late father had tapped him on the shoulder.

After *communing with the dead*, all the guests were invited to join Michaela who sat at the head of her large dining room table. Barbara had told us to bring a dish to share as a potluck meal, which was served by her houseboy. The dinners were fun. Michaela would regale us with charming stories of her life as a wildlife television host with Armand. She shared that spirits were attached to her house and told of a mischievous ghost who enjoyed hiding her car keys to play a prank on her. John and I enjoyed her charming and upbeat personality. It was amazing that she would invite near strangers to her beautiful home, and we felt blessed to be included in the fun.

On our last visit, we stood at her door to say goodbye and thank her for her hospitality. I was very pregnant at the time, and I asked if she had any thoughts as to what my baby might be. She looked at my swollen belly and announced that I would be having a boy. Her words sent a chill down my spine. I later thought it may have been my longing to give John his son, but I hoped she was correct. (Michaela Denis died in Nairobi, May, 2003 at age 88.)

After the last séance, my mother-in-law, Sue Allison, sent me a package with two outfits for a boy. She added a note that she had been to see a fortune teller who told her she would soon become the grandmother of a baby boy. The pressure was mounting, and I was getting nervous about the delivery.

At that time, baby showers were specifically an American custom, so I was touched when the ladies of Harlequins surprised me with a shower three weeks before my due date. I was presented with beautifully knitted blankets and sweaters handmade by the women. It was just one of the ways they wanted to make me feel loved—and I did.

October approached, and we were getting excited to finally welcome the newest member to our family. Doctor Papworth gave October 10, 1974, as my due date. It was the same date as

Chris Bane's' birthday, and Anita was hoping we might use that name if our child was a boy. In an odd coincidence, Josh chose to come October 12, an American holiday known as Christopher Columbus Day. Although I loved Christopher as a name, we chose Joshua, a name suggested by my father, Bruce, because he felt Josh Allison would make a good baseball name.

October 10 came with no movement. John and I were invited to go to dinner and to see Paul Newman and Robert Redford in *The Sting* the next night, October 11. The movie was outstanding, but halfway through I started to have labor pains. I did not want to miss the movie, so I decided not to tell John until we were in our car heading home. We got ready for bed and thinking I would be awake that night, I was surprised when I woke up the next morning after a peaceful night's sleep. Labor pains started up again mid-morning and continued off and on throughout the day. John had booked a time to play squash at Parklands Club, and I sent him off promising to call the club if the labor pains became more intense. I called the club at 5:00 PM and asked the man at the desk to relay a message for John to come home and take me to the hospital. The timing of the baby's arrival couldn't have been worse.

Early in my pregnancy, John had been given the honor of captaining the Harlequin rugby team for the 1974 season, and the annual Harlequin black-tie dinner was scheduled for that evening at the New Stanley Hotel. The all-male stag affair was steeped in tradition, and the captain's job was to give the keynote speech. There was pressure weighing on the speech, which was expected to be riddled with humorous anecdotes from the past season. John and I had been working on various ideas for weeks.

John called the previous year's captain, John Ellis, to let him know that he might be late for the affair. At that time, in England, it was not customary for husbands to hover over their wives in a hospital waiting for the delivery of a baby.

Ellis said, 'What are you thinking, mate? You can't do anything. Just drop Linda at the hospital and pitch up later after dinner to see how it all went. You have a speech to give, Captain, and it had better be funny.'

To John's credit, he declined this suggestion and said, 'In America, we stay with our wives until the baby is born. I will come to the dinner *after* Linda has the baby.'

When the girls had been born, John was told to sit with the other men in the waiting room, but times were changing, and men were encouraged to assist in the delivery room. I was wheeled into Mater Misericordiae Hospital at 6:00 PM with John by my side and greeted by a doctor I did not know.

'Dr. Papworth has been called away to assist with the Flying Doctors Service in northern Kenya. I will be delivering your baby,' explained an East Indian doctor I had never met. I was taken to the labor room, where an exceptionally large Kikuyu nurse promptly gave me a blazing hot enema.

I complained a little and she said, 'Hukuna matata, mama. Not to worry. This hot water will make your baby come upesi sana—very quick.'

I was dubious, but she knew what she was talking about. Things started moving extremely fast and within thirty minutes

I was in full labor and being wheeled into the delivery room. John noted that the time in the room was 6:30 PM.

Natural deliveries without drugs were the norm in England. I assumed that the natural approach would be the same for me. I had never delivered naturally. Therefore, I was surprised when the East Indian doctor stopped us at the door and said, 'There's a visiting doctor from America in the hospital demonstrating a new pain-reducing procedure called an epidural. He is here tonight. Would you like him to give you the injection?'

'YES!' I said in a relieved voice, and into the delivery room we went.

The delivery was moving forward rapidly. All of a sudden, the two attending Kenyan nurses looked at the clock. Noting that their shift was over, they walked out of the room. The doctor became frantic and shouted for help. An Irish nun, who happened by the door, came in to lend her assistance.

On October 12, 1974, a little after 7:00 PM, Joshua Scott Allison came into the world. He came out shooting a stream of pee into the air, and the doctor exclaimed, 'Good Lord! He's already spent a penny!'

John visited with me in my private room for thirty minutes before I encouraged him to get to the Harlequin dinner. I asked, 'Are you happy?'

'Linda, the miracle of birth is amazing. Uncontrollable tears were spilling down my cheeks. All I wanted was a healthy baby, but I must admit, I was never so happy to see a pair of balls in my life!'

It was a happy moment for our family. 'Go. Be with your team. It's 8:00 PM, and you have a speech to give.'

The next day, John reported that he had stopped off to buy a box of cigars before going to the hotel. 'I walked into the room with an enormous grin on my face. I didn't have to say a word and the men rose from their chairs and clapped for me. They just knew I had my son. It was something I'll never forget.'

With these formal rugby stag dinners, it is a long-standing tradition to serve steak and kidney pie as the entree. John did not care for steak and kidney pie.

'Linda, the best thing was when the waitress came over and apologized. She announced that they had run out of steak and kidney pie, and would I be happy with just a steak? I thought the evening couldn't get any better.'

'How did they like your speech?'

'The speech was very well received. I made them laugh. All in all, it was a perfect night.'

In San Diego, I stayed three days in the hospital with Shauna and Tara. A few years later my sister, Diane, was sent home the following day of the birth. In 1974, the practice in Kenya was for mother and baby to stay five days. My private room was the last in line and next to double doors leading to the maternity ward for Kenyan women. The country was encouraging hospital births for its women. I sighed when I heard the women laughing and talking in their ward, and thought, *This must be like a holiday for them. They appear to be having so much fun.*

In the evening, all the mothers would go to the nursery to get our babies for feeding. Josh had been the only Caucasian baby in the nursery, so he was always easy to find and carry back to my room. Josh was a beautiful baby, but he came out of the womb with a little squashed face. John and I lovingly teased that our baby looked like the cartoon character, Mister Magoo. Halfway down the corridor I saw the Kenyan women coming toward me from the ward chatting and smiling. I was looking at my baby thinking what a difference a day could make because his features had softened to an extremely sweet little face. Suddenly, I realized that this sweet-faced infant was *not* my baby. Unbeknownst to me an East Indian woman had given birth to a little girl that morning.

I let out a yelp and yelled, 'Oh goodness, this is not my baby!' An explosion of laughter erupted from the Kenyan women.

My face grew red, and I was convinced they were whispering to each other in Swahili, '*The stupid mzungu woman does not even know her baby.*' I was mortified when I had to turn and make my walk of shame back to the nursery to get my little guy. I picked him up and whispered, 'Yes, there is my little Mister Magoo.'

After my five-day stay at the hospital, John brought me home. Shauna, Tara, and our three workers, George, Chris, and Agnus, lined up at our kitchen door to greet me and meet our *little man*, whom they proudly called *bwana kidogo*.

'This name, Joshua, from the Old Testament, is very strong—enguvu sana,' offered George. 'You must be proud, bwana, to finally have your son to carry the ancestral name.'

John nodded and smiled as we passed through the kitchen door.

I felt like the Queen of England as I walked into a home that had been buffed and polished to a shine. The house seemed to sparkle, and it matched the mood of our little family. It was such a treat.

Within a week, our little Mister Magoo had lost his squished face and became an extremely cute baby and today is a dashingly handsome man.

Bwana Kidogo with houseboy George and ayah Agnus

Chapter 20:
1974 – An American Rugby Captain?

Harlequin Rugby club continued to be the primary foundation of our social life. Early in my pregnancy, John had come home with incredible news.

'Linda, you're never going to believe it, but the governing board voted me to captain the rugby team for the 1973-1974 season.'

'John, that's a tremendous honor. Has there ever been an American captain in Kenya?'

'I don't think so. I feel so honored.'

'You should be enormously proud. It's a testament to how the Harlequin players feel about you. I must say I'm a little surprised that the older members were on board with it.'

'Well, it may have ruffled a few knickers. Time will tell.'

As the previous year's captain and board member, John Ellis, later recounted, 'The only dissenting vote at the board meeting came from David Roundturner.'

David was an older non-playing member of the club who had chosen to stay in Kenya after it became a republic. We knew that David led tourists on safaris in Kenya and had always believed he was not fond of Americans. He had never warmed to us.

Ellis embellished the incident by adding, 'David's was the only dissenting vote in the room. We glared as Roundturner stood up, pounded his hand on the table, and voiced his disapproval to the board shouting; '*If the American, Allison, is voted in as our next captain, I will quit the club.*'

John Ellis said he pointed his index finger at the door and quipped, 'If you're not happy, David, you can take yourself up Ngong Road and join Impala Rugby Club. It's your choice, but Allison has the votes, and he *will* become our next captain.'

Roundturner was unhappy but decided to continue as a Harlequin, although he remained on chilly terms with the Allisons for the rest if our time in Kenya.

Voting John as captain was a testament to what the other players thought about him, and it was a tremendous honor. John brought a new perspective to the team's training program. As a high school coach and a lifelong athlete, John knew the importance of strength training. He initiated the idea of lifting weights at practice as a part of their fitness regimen.

KENYA HARLEQUIN F. C.
1st XV SEASON 1973-74
ENTERPRISE CUP FINALISTS

Standing: F.R. SMITH, M. FULLER, J.A. ELLIS, K. ROLLS, J. CASHIN, J.B. McFIE, J. MYER, B. MUKURIA, T. SIMPSON
Seated: D. LAWLESS, D.P. HAMILTON (Coach), J.A. ALLISON (Captain), F. GOSLING (Chairman), J. PLEWS (Vice Captain), K. KINYANJUI
C. BANE

John as captain of the 1973-74 Harlequin 1st XV Rugby Team

As Harlequin prop forward Chris Bane recently recalled to me:

> *In addition to weight training, John insisted on continuous training throughout the year, doing some type of disciplined sport when we were not playing rugby. That's where we got our first taste of cricket. I remember John striking out with the cricket bat because he used it as a baseball bat. When Coach Allison was able to get behind a cricket hit, it*

generally sailed out of the park because he was a powerful hitter, no doubt left over from early baseball days.

Coach Allison recruited four Kenyan players from NIS and because of his foresight, the Harlequins 1ˢᵗ XV included three Kenyans, four Americans including John as captain, with the rest of the team a mixture of English, Welsh, and Scottish players—a true international team thanks to John's efforts for inclusion of multiple nationalities.

John also encouraged the members to stay fit by playing squash, tennis, hiking, and running. After the regular season ended, two young Harlequin players and students at NIS, decided to climb Mount Kenya, which is 17,057 feet in elevation. This hike is no joke, and many mountain climbers fail to make it to the top due to exhaustion and altitude sickness.

While the boys were hiking, news came that Quins had been chosen to replace another team on a rugby tour. The Harlequin team was delighted to participate in the Seychelles, Reunion, and Madagascar tour. There was just one problem. John needed to find and retrieve two of his star players who were climbing Mount Kenya.

Mark Wiley and Craig Hunter were coming down off Lenana Peak (16,335 feet) and were stunned to see Coach Allison and Bill Stanley, who had come to fetch them for the tour. After a quick gathering of supplies, all four of them ran down the mountain so they could prepare for the tour. John later told me that he was in such decent shape that he and young Bill charged up the mountain without any strain in order to fill the team roster.

Nairobi International School had an agreement with the Kenyan government to award scholarships to a certain percentage of young boys and girls from Nairobi. In 1971, John was building his sports program in soccer, basketball, track and field, and rugby. John saw promise in a tall Nairobi boy named Frank Matsalia who had never played organized sports.

Recently, Frank shared his memories with me:

> *So much about Coach Allison is much like it happened yesterday. I attended the US community school in late 1969 as the only Kenyan student. It was not until the school relocated to Kitsuru that it felt like home. The biggest contributor to that feeling was Coach Allison. He was the sports wing for the whole school. I was interested, so I joined a soccer gathering one afternoon. I was picked to be an integral member of the first soccer team at NIS. It was the only organized sports entity I had ever been a part of. Each sport figured me as a big part of it because of Coach Allison's urging. He saw in me what I had never seen in myself, excelling in sports as part of who I was. By the time he introduced rugby to the*

school I had so much confidence in my athletic abilities, it was only a question of where to play, who, and when. During all this, Coach Allison himself became a member of the Kenya Harlequin's rugby club. Of course, several of us at the high school were 'recruited' by Coach to play for the club. One afternoon during rugby practice came a sound like a firecracker. It was a bone from Bill Stanley's shin breaking! Coach Allison immediately had him bite on a stick to prevent him from biting his tongue off and also to prevent shock. His quick action calmed us all down. Another time, I had a minor swelling in the small of my back. I remember showing it to him. He examined it and made an appointment with his personal physician the following Saturday to have it professionally examined. It turned out to be nothing serious, but Coach was like a father figure to many of us. Not just the greatest coach.

During this time, John was recruiting NIS boys like Frank Matsalia, Mark Wiley, Chris Bane, and Craig Hunter to play for Harlequin's. There were very few Kenyan players in the rugby clubs. Through John's insight and effort, other clubs began opening the game up to Kenyan boys. Today, Harlequin's Rugby Club is thriving. All of its players are young, fit, and athletic Kenyan Africans.

John was also invited to participate in a Combined Kenya, Tanzania, and Uganda Rugby Union *All East Africa Zambia Tour*. By this time, John was fully engaged in the traditions of the rugby clubs. One tradition he came to love was after a scrappy and fiercely competitive match, the players would celebrate with beer and song.

At one of our social events at the club, John approached me with an idea we had seen on The Johnny Carson Show. A comedian performed an absurd magic act using only his fingers and a few silly props. The act was so ridiculous that it was hysterical to watch.

The comedian began by humming a simple melody of, da da da da, da da da da da, over and over and then went into his act. As an example, the comedian would hold up two clinched fists and show the audience that there was nothing hidden behind them. He would then bang them together and on his right hand, his index finger would *mysteriously* pop straight up in the air. He would continue humming and banging them together with fingers flying and popping up in different configurations. He then put his index fingers and thumbs together to form two circles. He knocked the two circles together demonstrating there were no hidden breaks. He then put the circles behind his head and when he lifted them to the front the circles were *mysteriously* connected. He encouraged the audience to cheer at his crazy antics. It was stupid and silly and that's what made it so ridiculously funny.

John and I felt that this comedic skit would be a tremendous hit with the rugby group. We practiced for a week and added a few of our own silly ideas to the act. The spoof was received with overwhelming enthusiasm, and John was asked to perform it on various occasions. The *All-East Africa Zambia Tour* was set to go, and the players prodded John to perform the skit after all their rugby games to executives, elected officials, and teams from various countries.

John came home and said, 'I performed that act before governors and dignitaries. It was incredible, and they all loved it. Harlequin members, who eventually left Kenya, asked John if they could borrow the *Magic Act*. Just as Bob Shepherd had gifted him *The Lobster Song*, John was delighted to *gift* the act to Rob Evans in London, John Maynard in South Africa, and other players who had given him so much.

Rugby can be a brutal sport. After several seasons, John had moved from the wing position to become a prop forward. In rugby, two prop forwards are positioned in the front row of the scrum to assist the middleman or hooker, whose job is to kick the ball backwards through the scrum to the number nine player, called a scrum half, waiting to retrieve and lateral the ball out to the backfield positions. Being a prop forward was a taxing and very physical position and John loved being in the middle of the fray.

During the Zambia tour, a big Irish prop forward named Duffy continually attempted to gouge John in the eye while in the scrum. Duffy was notorious for being an aggressive player, and the team had been cautioned about him. John warned Duffy to knock the antics off, but the dirty tricks continued. John decided to bide his time so he could exact revenge. He waited until the teams were standing next to each other in a lineout. The idea of a lineout is much like a jump-ball in basketball. A player stands outside the sideline and throws the rugby ball up in the air to both teams who are formed into two lines. The men jump and are sometimes hoisted in the air by their teammates in an effort to tap the ball to their side of the team.

John waited, and when the ball was tossed and the line of men rose in the air, John reached across the line and knocked Duffy out with a sly right uppercut to the jaw. In the ensuing confusion, and all eyes focused on the ball, no one knew what had happened. The big Irishman lay unconscious on the grass. The referee blew his whistle and Duffy was carried off the pitch. The game continued without officials knowing what had happened to the Irishman, and John wasn't talking.

Later that night at the tour dinner, John remained coy. He had made his point and that was all that needed doing. The Zambia team huddled in small groups to talk about the game. John said he could hear players gesticulating and speculating over the continuing theme of *who duffed Duffy.*

In 1975, John received a special honor and was awarded an *Honours Cap* by Harlequin Rugby Club for his outstanding play and leadership commitment to the club. It was another validation of his teammates' respect for him as a player.

Rugby Honours Caps are presented to players who represent their club and country with distinction. Its history dates back to 1839 at Rugby School where the boys wore crimson velvet caps with gold tassels. Initially, it was part of the team uniform but later became an award in recognition of rugby players who exemplify its ideals and dedication to the sport. Today, Honours Caps are worn to dinner ceremonies and other dedicated events.

Chapter 21:
1974 – A Christening at Christmas

My parents, Bruce and Esther Shields, flew out for Christmas, 1974. Together, we drove to Eldoret to have Joshua Scott baptized, with my parents stepping in as godparents. John and I, along with Shauna and Tara, looked on as our dear friends Father Patrick Scanlon and Father Terry Nash officiated the ceremony in the church.

Father Scanlon began asking the litany of baptismal questions, which the godparents and family answer for the baby as our profession of faith, with the words: 'I do.'

'Do you renounce Satan.'

'I do.'

'And all his empty promises.'

'I do.'

As the litany of questions continued, Father Nash grew enthusiastic in his responses and began saying in his robust Irish accent, 'I do now! I do now!'

Later, Mom shared that she got quite the kick out of the young priest's emphatic rejection of Satan and all his evil works and empty promises. We combined the trip to Eldoret with my parents to include a trip to Naro Moru near Mount Kenya. We rented a cabin and spent several relaxing days watching John and Bruce teach Tara and Shauna to fish for trout in the river.

Shauna learning to fish for trout at Naro Moru

**Enjoying time with Mom and Josh at
Parklands Club in Nairobi**

After the Christmas festivities, John and my dad went on a camping safari with fellow teacher, Tom Simpson, to Buffalo Springs, while Mom and I enjoyed the pool at Parklands and shopping in the city. Tom Simpson had joined the many young Americans who answered President Kennedy's call to join the Peace Corp. Tom was sent to Kenya where he met and later married, Agnes, a beautiful Kalenjin girl who lived near the slopes of Mount Elgon. After his service was completed, Tom joined NIS as part of the teaching staff.

Almost immediately upon their return, another teacher from NIS, Bob Mazelow, invited my dad and John to attend a rite of passage called a Masai Inota in the Kajiado area of Kenya where the nomadic Masai tribe was staying. The opportunity was too great an event to pass up and one rarely attended by those outside the tribe. Bob graciously shared his memories of the event with me:

> *The Masai Inota ceremony lasts about four days and culminates with the young men advancing from warriors to junior elders in their tribe. There is much singing and dancing and lots of drinking by the elders. Masai do not eat their cattle except during festivals or ceremonies. They get their protein by draining blood from the cattle's jugular vein, mixing it in a gourd with milk and human urine for consumption. After four days of celebration, a ceremonial cutting of their long dreadlock hair is the climax of the event. The hair is cut with a razor and red ochre clay is rubbed onto the scalp. After the Inota ceremony, the boys take their place as junior elders in the tribe and soon after will become betrothed to a young bride.*

My father, John, and Bob were amazed at how athletic the warriors were. The young men loved to gather and jump high into the air from a standing position. They invited Bob to wrestle some of the boys and asked John to participate in a game of strength.

John in a game of strength with the Masai Warriors. To honor John, the warriors invited him to wear an ostrich feather headdress for a group photo.

The Masai warriors were intrigued by the blond hair on John's arms and wanted to run their hands over it. At this time, John had been playing rugby and lifting weights and was fit and strong. Several of the warriors challenged him to a game of strength, which is a similar version of arm wrestling. John was told to extend his arm out straight and a warrior would try and push his arm down toward the ground. Each time a warrior challenged him, John was able to resist and break free to lift his arm upward toward the sky. The young men were amazed at his strength. John invited three warriors to grasp his outstretched arm and try to push it downward, but they couldn't. The young men were so impressed, they insisted John wear a ceremonial headdress of ostrich feathers and take a photo with them.

Masai are particular about having their photo taken, as they believe you are taking part of their soul or spirit. If you are a good person and ask, they may give their permission to allow one to take a photo. The young warriors lined with graduation poses to have my dad snap a photo with John. Later, John and my dad said that the ceremony was the trip of a lifetime.

John and Bruce also participated in an unusual piece of Kenya history. In 1973, Jomo Kenyatta banned game hunting for elephants and the ivory trade. Renowned artist, Davis Schaefer, had procured a hunting license, which needed to be used before midnight December 31, 1974, or he would lose the licensing money paid to secure the plot of land for the shoot. Although John did not enjoy hunting game in Kenya, he could not pass up the opportunity to be a part of history when Schaefer invited Bruce and John to photograph the hunt. Days passed with no success. Late in the afternoon on December 31, 1974 David was able to bring down a large bull elephant. The event marked the last legal elephant hunt in Kenya.

Bruce photographing John and David Schaefer, on the last legal elephant hunt in Kenya

We said goodbye to my parents with plans to meet during our home leave in the summer of 1975. Our plans would change, but we were unaware at the time.

We loved living in our new house and were thrilled to welcome our baby boy. Things were going well—until they were not. Events were changing rapidly with the CIA. Our mentor, Howard Bane, and his family had been posted to The Hague. Fred departed soon after but told us we would be assigned a new case manager who would become our handler.

Fred wanted to take his beloved collection of Playboy magazines, but was worried about excess baggage, so he sold us two small Zanzibar chests for fifty dollars each. It was a fair price, and we have enjoyed having them in our family for years as a reminder of Fred. Over our time with the CIA, we developed a real sense of friendship with Fred and Howard. We knew they genuinely cared about us and wanted the best for us. We were treated with kindness and respect in all our dealings with them. It came as a surprise to us that our new handler was so different.

Soon after Fred's departure, we were assigned a new case manager named Jay. One Sunday, he invited us over to his house to meet his wife, whose name escapes me. Jay's wife was very docile and a little shy. Together, they had a young three-year-old daughter. From the start, I could see she took a back seat in their family dynamics. We had met Jay once and John and I felt the meeting had been a little strained. When Jay invited us to his home for a barbecue, John and I were hoping to make a better impression.

Jay was a young brash agent and appeared to have a chip on his shoulder. In our initial meeting with him, he let us know that he was in charge of things and running the show. John and I wondered if he did not like our close relationship with the former Chief of Station in the agency. More importantly, judging from his behavior toward his wife, I suspected Jay had an issue with women in general. The barbecue went fine, but I had an uncomfortable view of Jay, which made me nervous.

Jay was an avid rock climber and one weekend he invited us to join him and his sweet wife and daughter on a picnic and rock-climbing excursion at a place he frequented outside the city. He offered to take us in his big Land Rover. It soon became clear he had an ulterior motive.

In retrospect, I thought Jay wanted to show off a bit for John and put him in his place. Jay knew that John played rugby and was an accomplished athlete. He never explained what equipment or clothing John should bring or wear. John showed up in rugby shorts, a tee shirt, and regular training shoes. The girls and I piled into the back of the Land Rover with Jay's wife and daughter. Jay told John to take the passenger seat.

At that time, I was in my third trimester of pregnancy and was really showing. As Jay took the Rover off-roading, he seemed to get a weird sense of enjoyment driving the vehicle fast and tossing us out of our seats over the ruts and bumps. I was grabbing onto anything I could get ahold of as I bounced six inches off the seat and into the air. I thought it was extremely impolite of Jay, but decided I would not give him the satisfaction of asking him to slow down for me.

After twenty minutes of this nonsense, his wife asked in a timid voice, 'Jay, could you go slower? We have a very pregnant woman in the car, and we're being jostled about back here.'

John looked back at me with a concerned look in his eyes, and asked how I was doing. I shook my head, and he also requested that Jay take it slower.

At this time, John had been playing rugby and was extremely fit, but he was not prepared to climb with improper equipment. When we reached our destination, Jay promptly got himself rigged up with climbing boots, gloves, and long pants, things he never suggested or had brought for John to wear. Jay prepared to climb the cliff, attaching his harness to clips already imbedded in the rock. We all looked on as he scaled the forty-foot cliff. He rappelled down, gave John a few pointers, and told John to give it a go.

John had never climbed, but he said he was up for the challenge. I was annoyed. To me, Jay wanted John to fail. Without proper equipment or clothing, John began to scale the cliff. He got about halfway to the top before stopping to catch his breath. I could see he was really struggling. His shoes kept slipping off the rock, but I knew he would give it his best.

Jay yelled, 'You can't stop now! If you're going to be a rock climber you must make it all the way to the top. A climber doesn't quit.'

I became nervous. It was clear that Jay had placed John in a dangerous situation. I felt I could almost read what John was thinking, but I knew he would not back down from the challenge. Primarily using arm strength, John pulled his body to the top of the cliff. I believe Jay had wanted John to fail, although I didn't know why. To establish a pecking order? Perhaps because of our close relationship with the former Chief of Station and his family.

Later, on our way home from the outing, I asked John, 'What was that all about? Jay put you in a dangerous situation. I was really proud that you made it up the side of the cliff.'

John had an easy-going nature and got along well with most people. Therefore, I chuckled when John said, 'That guy's a dick!'

I laughed and said, 'I agree. I'm worried having Jay as our handler.'

'I'm not certain what his motive was, but I wasn't going to give him the satisfaction of seeing me fail. It was all arms there at the end, Linda. I'm going to be sore tomorrow. Plus, I was more annoyed with the way he was driving with you in the car. I think we're going to miss Fred.'

The rock-climbing event foreshadowed what life would be for us over our remaining time in Kenya. After months of weighing the pros and cons of joining the CIA, John and I became convinced we had made the right decision for him to continue teaching.

It was a decision that turned out in our favor. The policies of the agency had come into question and a complete revamping and downsizing of the firm led to many people being let go. We felt that we would have been in that first wave, being on the bottom rung of the ladder.

So many of the people we had worked with for the past two years were no longer with the agency in Nairobi. We continued to do small jobs—clear the house for safe meetings—get mail from various post boxes and entertain various clients when asked. However, with the influx of new agents, we did not have the rapport we once had with the agency.

Chapter 22:
1975/1976 – Changing Tides and Travel

We had fulfilled our second two-year teaching contract with NIS and were entitled to another home leave with NIS paying for roundtrip fares for our family of five. We had said goodbye to my parents at Christmas, with the promise to see them in the summer of 1975, but our plans would soon change.

John's mother, Sue, said she would like to come for a visit to see her new grandson. As she had never come out to see us, we thought it only fair that we show her around Kenya. We asked NIS if we could decline the trip home and instead take the stipend, which amounted to about five thousand dollars, and enjoy our vacation in Kenya. The school agreed.

Up until this time, our safari trips had been on a budget, with camping being our main amenity. On occasion, we would be reimbursed when asked to spy for the CIA at one of the lodges, but those opportunities were rare. With a little extra money in our pockets, we decided to treat Sue to a proper tourist-style holiday. We booked lodging in Tsavo National Game Park and spent several days touring the park, watching the giraffes, zebras, and the enormous herds of elephants roaming the savanna. Sue was delighted to see Kenya from the luxury of game lodges and hotels.

I will never forget the sight of a fallen elephant on the flat savanna of Tsavo game park. Six or eight other elephants hovered in a circle guarding it. The herd made mournful sounds as the surrounding group of elephants tried to coax the dying female to her feet. We parked our car at a respectful distance. A ranger came over and explained that the elephant had been sick and was dying of natural causes. He shared that elephants are so heavy that they cannot lie down for too long as their lungs will collapse. We watched the ritual in helpless fascination until Tara, who had always been sensitive to animals, asked if we could leave the area.

We decided to visit the hippopotamuses at Mzima Springs. On our way into the park the previous day, we had stopped at the springs just at dusk and before checking into our rooms. Hippos are nocturnal creatures and love to feed on various plants at night. They were just beginning to stir from their restful day of slumber. The giant mammals delighted us by raising their heads out of the water and emitting a guttural honking sound, similar to the braying of a donkey, from their large open mouths.

The next day we returned to Mzima Springs. John wanted to take a Super 8-Millimeter action video of the hippos. My parents had purchased a camera for us while living in Japan. We brought it to Kenya and would send them movies so they could be a part of our journey and record the growth of the girls. These early video cameras did not have sound but gave them an idea of our lives in Kenya. I know they looked forward to receiving these updates.

It was the middle of the day as we stood near the shore watching a large herd of hippos resting in the springs with only their ears and noses peeking above the water. John tried waving his hands and calling out to entice them to *Do Something*. But the hippos ignored his antics and rested in peaceful slumber.

'John, I have an idea.

'What are you thinking?'

'Remember when we were here at dusk and the hippos were raising their heads and making those guttural sounds with their mouths open?'

John looked at me and said, 'Yeah. It appeared as though they were waking up and getting ready to forage for food. But I don't remember what they sounded like.'

'That's the thing. I do, and I think I might be able to replicate it.'

Shauna and Tara started jumping up and down saying, 'Do it, Mommy! Make the hippos come up out of the water.'

The problem was, we were standing at a lookout point watching the hippos from a river that fed into the springs and there was a group of tourists standing next to us.

I lowered my voice and said, 'I will try to make the sound girls, but we must be patient. There are other people around. Let's wait for them to leave and mommy will try and make the hippo call.' Tara put her hands on her hips and stared at the group with a funny scowl on her face. She clapped when the group left to board their bus.

John readied his camera for the video shot. I opened my mouth, cupped my hands, and discharged the call as loudly and as closely as I could remember it sounding. To our shock and utter amazement, the entire herd of thirty hippos rose their sleepy heads up out of the water, looked around in all directions, and after a few seconds, slowly sank their heads into the water.

'Oh my God, Linda, that was amazing, and I got the action shot of them looking around.'

I looked over at John's mother, Sue, who was holding Josh. She was smiling. The girls began jumping up and down, while shouting, 'Do it again, Mommy! Do it again!'

I coughed and said, 'That was fun, but mommy's throat is kind of hurt.'

Throughout the course of my teaching elementary students in Hemet, I always finished the year with a unit on Kenya—using slides and film my father had gathered and copied on to a VCR tape. When I showed them the silent movie of the sleeping herd of hippos, I would pause the film and ask them if they would like me to make the hippo call that tricked an entire herd to rise up from the river. My students loved it, but the guttural sound was hard on my vocal cords!

Traveling with Sue south to Mombasa, we spent two nights at the stately Nyali Beach Hotel, founded in 1946 as Mombasa's first proper hotel on the mainland. The hotel reflected the gracious style of that period and offered world-class cuisine. On our last night at the hotel, John's mother Sue and our family of five dined on an exquisite meal on a patio veranda overlooking the Indian Ocean. The heat of the day had abated, and we lingered to enjoy the stars twinkling above the ocean on the balmy night.

After dinner, our servers invited all the guests to sample a spectacular dessert table set up in the middle of the patio. My eyes were drawn to a towering cone shaped dessert made from balls of cream puffs filled with whipped cream and held together with a chocolate ganache and crystallized caramel dripping down its sides. I had never seen anything like it in my life. My mother had often made cream puffs for dessert, but nothing like this. I extricated two cream puffs from the tower and walked back to our table. Not only was the dessert a sight to behold, but the texture of the choux pastry filled with whipped cream, fudgy chocolate, and crystallized caramel was a delight to eat. It was soft, creamy, and crunchy—and I had to figure out how to make it.

Luckily, Harlequin wife, Margaret Hamilton, had a recipe and generously shared it with me. Over the years, I have often replicated the dessert, and my guests are always delighted in the combination of its delicate and unusual textures and flavors.

We journeyed north on the coastal road along the Indian Ocean to Malindi. It was fun to be a little extravagant and see Kenya as a tourist. We visited our favorite hotel in Malindi and booked two rooms at the Mnarani Beach Club. The old hotel was a favorite of locals and tourists. With Grandma Sue and the girls occupying one room, and John, Josh, and myself in the other, we enjoyed the beach and the hotel pool. It was a relaxing vacation and one we never regretted. We were delighted to be able to show John's mother Kenya through the eyes of a tourist.

Upon our arrival back in Nairobi, we were notified that we would need to vacate the safe house one evening, By this time we were well prepared for reasons why we and our visiting guests needed to spend a few hours away from the house.

During our first four years in the city, there were no fast-food restaurants available to us. Therefore, we were delighted when a chicken franchise was built off the Nairobi Expressway near Westlands. We popped out of the house for a little *fast food*, which delighted the girls.

After showing Sue what our life in Nairobi was like, we sadly bid farewell to her and began preparing for our fifth-year teaching at Nairobi International School.

We continued to do small jobs for the CIA, but nearly every agent who had a connection with Howard had moved on to a different assignment in a different country. It became clear that the new wave of agents at the embassy didn't know who we were. Also, it was clear that our new handler, Jay, was not a fan. We couldn't understand why Jay felt as he did, but we continued to appreciate the guidance of our previous handler, Fred. Although small in stature and not your typical archetype of a secret agent, we came to appreciate his steadfast work ethic and obvious love for his country.

We continued to receive a monthly stipend in Kenyan shillings and the American dollars, which were deposited in our bank account in San Diego. It was money we never touched or really thought about. It was just there.

✻ ✻ ✻ ✻ ✻ ✻

In November of 1975, I received a letter from my father, Bruce, who wanted to surprise my mother and sister by flying me to San Diego for my sister Diane and her fiancé Buddy's wedding on January 10, 1976. Bruce graciously offered to pay for half the airfare if John and I could produce the balance.

John understood that I had not seen my younger sister in over four years, and I wanted to support her on her wedding day. He was happy to agree to the trip, although it meant being away from him and the girls for six weeks.

Two obstacles arose. We were told that a married woman could not leave Nairobi without her husband's permission, and I planned to take Josh, but he didn't have a passport.

I won't lie. I was a little annoyed about the permission thing, but Kenya was behind the times in terms of women's rights. John happily gave the necessary permission for me to leave the country without him, and the American embassy facilitated us in attaching a photo of Josh to Shauna and Tara's existing passport.

To save money in 1971, the girls' passport photo was taken together, and they were able to travel on it as long as they did so together. This is a practice not allowed anymore. To expedite our trip to San Diego, the embassy attached another photo of Josh to the girls' passport, but because his photo was separate from theirs, he was able to travel with me alone.

 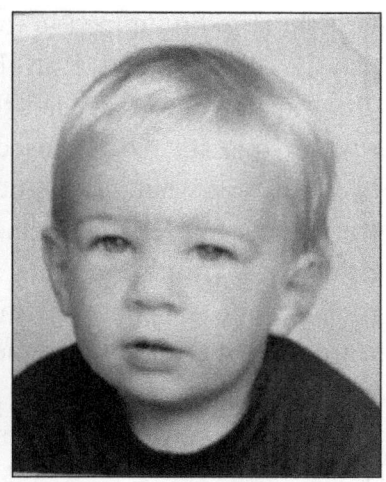

Passport Photos of Shauna, Tara (1971) and Josh (1975)

Before my scheduled flight to San Diego, we had planned a trip over Christmas to stay at the Mnarani Beach Club in Malindi with Rob and Sue Evans, and a German couple, who were non-playing members of Harlequins, Rolf and Sylke Schmidt. We always had great fun with our friends, but this trip was memorable for several unfortunate incidents, all of which we laughed about later.

Together with Rob and Sue Evans, we had become friendly with a young German couple who had recently joined the club as non-playing members. We invited the new members to join us for a Christmas holiday at the Mnarani Club in Malindi.

Rolf always wore glasses. Early in our stay, he and Rob were snorkeling in a rocky cove observing some beautiful tropical fish. Rolf asked John if he would hold his glasses while he snorkeled. John put them in his shirt pocket and promptly forgot about them. Rolf and Rob were oohing and ahhing over the fish, so John jumped in to have a look. In the process, he lost the glasses, and Rolf had not brought another pair. Unfortunately, Rolf needed the glasses to correct a type of severe astigmatism that caused his right pupil to flair out to the side. Rolf was what one might call a stereotypical German. He was a man of order and the incident with the glasses made the trip miserable for him.

We rented a house on the Mnarani property with three bedrooms. Sue woke up in the morning covered in welts. We discovered that her mattress was riddled with bedbugs. We dragged the mattress into the sun for a day and that solved the issue.

During the course of one evening while sitting under the stars, the six friends suddenly realized that our fathers had fought in WWII for Britain, Germany, and the United States. Yet, here we were, the offspring of that horrific time, sharing a wonderful friendship. It was interesting to discuss the events of our fathers in relation to their war experiences.

Rolf said. 'I was lucky to have been born because Hitler sent my father to the Russian front. My father said the conditions were horrific, and he was dying of cold and hunger. In a desperate move my father shot himself in the leg during a battle with the Russian army. He was taken back to Germany, which saved his life. I believe my father lived with the guilt of his action, but most of his unit died during that campaign.'

We asked how Hitler was portrayed in historical context at school. He replied that his teachers seemed to place more of the blame on Hitler's henchmen, Martin Bormann, Heinrich

Himmler and Josef Mengele. His assessment of this was interesting to me and I pondered it a lot.

Rob, who was older and remembered the war, shared that he was five and walking down a road with other children near London when a German plane flew low and strafed bullets onto the street. 'Many children on the opposite side of the road were hit and killed. It could have easily been me, if I had been in the wrong place. I just got lucky.'

One afternoon, the club offered a cold luncheon buffet for the guests. Everyone but Rob and I got food poisoning from something they ate. Our kids had been excited to go to a party to meet Father Christmas. The infected members of our group writhed in misery at our rental house as Rob and I took the girls to a children's Christmas party put on by the club.

A lot of our time was spent sunbathing and swimming at the hotel's large pool. For some reason the water was murky, but the employees assured us that the pool was perfectly safe for swimming. The water was so cloudy that one could not see the bottom of the pool, but no one got sick, so we decided to take a chance. We had been swimming in the pool for days.

Despite continuous warnings, our fourteen-month-old Josh kept venturing near the edge of the pool and one of us would race over to save him from falling in. John had an idea to teach him a lesson with a little scare.

'Linda, I believe that if Josh understood the danger, he would be more careful about what might happen if he were to fall in the water.'

'Okay. What were you thinking?'

'I want you to position yourself in the deep end of the pool and tread water. I will drop Josh into the pool and when he pops to the top you can grab him. I believe the experience will help him understand the danger of the pool.'

With our friends and other guests at the pool watching, John held Josh by his arms and gently dropped him into the cloudy pool. I waited for Josh to bob to the surface. Nothing. It felt like minutes, but it was probably only seconds, but nevertheless a very few tense moments ensued. I was flailing my feet and hands to feel where he was, but the water was too murky to see anything. I was becoming frantic and so were our friends and other onlookers. John didn't want to jump in the pool because he feared he might land on the little guy. Eventually, Josh bobbed to the surface and was fine. All who witnessed the incident breathed a sigh of relief and we all went back to enjoying the day. Josh, however, continued to stray to the edge of the pool, so the lesson had been not only stupid, but scary and fruitless.

Several weeks later, we were at Parklands swimming pool in Nairobi enjoying a Sunday swim. A man came up to John and said, 'You look familiar to me. I think I know you.'

John answered, 'No, I don't believe we have ever met.'

All of a sudden, the man snapped his fingers and shouted, 'I remember you. I know who you are.'

'You do?'

'Yes. You're that dumb American bloke who dropped his baby in the deep end of the pool at the Mnarani Club! We all thought you were crazy.'

An embarrassed John replied, 'Yes, I guess that wasn't what you might call one of my brightest ideas.'

One interesting coincidence happened on the trip that Christmas. As a rule, John was easy-going. My dad loved John, but would often say to me, 'John leaves a lot to chance.' It was very true and defined the way he lived his life. It was also true that objects sometimes found their way back to him. I will share a few uncanny incidents here.

Once, shortly after we had married, John was working at a Chevron Station in Pacific Beach when a couple came in for gas. They handed him a credit card that bore John's name on it. It looked like his card, but he considered there might be another John Allison in San Diego. John went inside the pay station and called me to verify the credit card number. I happened to be paying bills at the time and quickly verified it was his card. Apparently, it had been stolen from his glove compartment while he was student-teaching some fifteen miles away at Grossmont High School. In fact, John didn't know the card was missing. He casually mentioned that he was having trouble processing the card on the machine and it would just be a few minutes. As the couple waited, John called the police. The couple were arrested, and his credit card was returned to him.

Another time, while pumping gas at a station in Point Loma, John saw a kid pull up to a red stop light in a car that looked a lot like the one he had parked behind the gas station with his keys in it. John excused himself from his customer and approached the young man behind the wheel waiting for the light to turn green and said, 'Son, this is my car. I recognize my books in the back seat. I suggest you pull it back into that driveway, park it, and walk away. No questions asked. If you drive away, when that light turns green, I will call the cops, and you will be arrested.' The young man guiltily nodded and replaced the car where he had stolen it.

John had played professional baseball in the minor leagues for the Dodger organization. On home leave in 1973 John asked a friend, still connected with the Dodgers, to purchase an official fitted Dodger hat for him. He did, and John was thrilled when he received it.

The New Era Company had been making official baseball hats for its professional players for decades. In the 1980s, New Era began selling authentic team-branded hats to fans with tremendous success. Today any fan can buy a fitted hat of their favorite team, but this was not the case in the seventies. It was unusual to own an officially fitted hat from a professional team. John loved the LA Dodger hat, but unfortunately, it was stolen from the back of our car in Nairobi in the fall of 1973. He accepted that he would never see it again, but fate intervened.

At Malindi, there was nothing that resembled a Christmas tree anywhere along the coast, and we wanted to have some type of tree to place the kid's gifts under. Sue, Sylke and I asked the guys to search the countryside to see if they could find anything in the shape of a Christmas tree. John told the story to me later that day.

'We drove down a dirt road where we saw sisal trees in the distance and came to a village of Kenyans a few miles south of our hotel. The villagers were surprised to see us, because it was not a place tourists would have a reason to go. We got out of our car to ask if we might purchase a sisal plant. A few members of the tribe spoke English and agreed to cut one down for us. A young teenage boy came up to us, and to my surprise, he had my LA Dodger hat on his head! I was shocked, Linda. I was so surprised that without thinking, I plucked the hat off his head.'

I quickly turned to Rob and Rolf and announced, 'Hey guys, this is my LA Dodger hat. It was stolen from the back seat of my car about two years ago. This is so weird. I thought I'd never see it again.'

I shook my head and asked, 'What did you do?'

'The young boy got a little nervous, so I assured him I didn't want the hat back. In truth, it was pretty beat up and dirty. So, I plunked it back on his head and asked where he had gotten it, but he either didn't understand or couldn't remember.'

'That's amazing, John. That village near Malindi is a seven-hour drive from Nairobi. How did it get from the back of our car to that remote village? What a story the hat could tell.'

'I can't believe I saw it again, and in a place I never should have been.'

'Yes. You lose things, but they find a way of coming back to you.'

* * * * * *

The time came to say goodbye to John and the girls to attend my sister's wedding in San Diego. It was another long trip home. To save money, Josh was allowed to travel free as long as he sat on my lap during full flights. As luck would have it, every seat was taken on both flights. The twenty-two-hour trip to Los Angelas via Paris was grueling with little sleep for us both. I longed for the overhead hammock used by Tara on our first charter flight to London, but those had been declared unsafe and had been recently banned by the airlines.

I was exhausted and sore as we passed through customs in Los Angeles. From there, I had to walk from the international terminal of LAX to the domestic section of the airport. The airport was huge and the distance long. In 1976 there were no roller wheels on suitcases to move luggage, no airport carts to transfer a young mother and her fifteen-month-old toddler to another terminal. I was coming for a six-week stay and had two large suitcases, a carry-on bag, a handbag, and a long way to go to make my connecting flight to San Diego. Fifteen-month-old Josh was tired and only wanted to sit down. I began to panic until I thought of the BALL.

Josh had been around rugby and soccer his entire young life. He began walking at nine months and had been watching his dad coach sports from the time he could sit up. He knew his way around all types of balls.

At a recent Harlequins game, I followed him as he toddled down to the pitch during halftime. I became intrigued as he picked up a large rugby ball left on the sideline and walked to the middle of the rugby pitch. I felt no harm could come to him, so I stayed on the sideline and watched to see what he wanted to do. People in the stands began to take notice of the young toddler who had walked onto the middle of the pitch with a rugby ball in his hands. I had no idea what his purpose was, but as I looked up into the stands, I noticed several more people standing, clearly entertained, and intrigued by the toddler with the rugby ball. With a solemn and intent expression on his face, Josh turned toward the goal post, banged his heel in an effort to gouge an indentation in the grass, which is what a kicker did to *make his mark*. After several attempts to make the ball remain upright—success. Josh then stepped methodically back five paces before taking one step to the left. I was surprised that he knew how to do this, exactly as he had seen his father prepare to kick a goal. Josh studied the situation before charging at the ball. He made contact and kicked it five yards dribbling along the grass. Everyone in the stands began clapping and cheering at the little toddler kicking the ball. Josh was aware of the cheering, so he did it again. Soon, it became a regular halftime exhibition at the home games.

American children grow up throwing a ball, but in England, Europe, and Kenya, young boys grow up kicking a ball, and Josh was no exception. During soccer season, Josh could be seen running up and down the sidelines mimicking the boys on the field kicking the ball. In fact, his very first sentence was, 'Kick the ball.' Josh just didn't kick the ball; he could control the ball as he moved it along the grass, just as he mimicked the soccer players on the field.

Suddenly, I remembered that Josh had gotten an inexpensive plastic/rubber ball from Czechoslovakia for Christmas, about the size of a small melon. I retrieved the colorful ball from my carry-on luggage and placed it in front of him hoping he would cooperate. Josh perked up and began kicking the ball down the walkway, like a seasoned soccer player dribbling the ball down field. People proceeding along the corridor moved aside for him and were commenting among each other.

'Look at that little kid!'

'Can you believe the way that young boy can control that ball?'

'I've never seen anything like it!'

I breathed a sigh of relief. *Kicking the Ball* became a fun game for Josh, and we covered the distance to our awaiting plane in record time.

My sister Diane and Buddy's wedding was the highlight of our visit. Buddy's sister stepped back and graciously let me take the role of matron of honor. Fortunately, we found a matching dress in my size, and I was able to be a part of their beautiful day.

The six weeks flew by in a flurry of activity. We enjoyed spending time at a family vacation house my dad had built in Ensenada, Mexico. Mom and Dad were excited to take me to the San Diego Wild Animal Park, which had opened in May 1972. About halfway through the excursion, Dad turned to me and said, 'This can't be that exciting for you. You live in the real thing.'

I told him no. 'The people of San Diego have always been proud of our zoo and safari park. I'm happy to see it has expanded to this new facility.'

It was a wonderful visit, but I was excited to return home to John and the girls. This time, Dad offered to drive me to Los Angeles to catch the first leg of my flight to France and then Kenya. It's always a sad farewell to say goodbye to loved ones. We shared a final meal together at the iconic LAX restaurant.

My father seemed unusually melancholy as we ate. I offered. 'Don't be sad, Dad. John and I will see you soon.'

I had always understood how much Bruce loved Kenya. He looked up from his meal and surprised me by saying, 'Linda, I think I would like to visit Kenya one more time. I don't believe your mother wants to go, but I have to see it again. I hope your mother will understand.'

'I think she will, Dad. You have always been so generous about Mom's trips with her lady friends to visit Hong Kong and Korea to shop. Dad, I would love for you to come, and I know John would love it too.'

The talk of another visit made my trip back to Kenya less sad, and I looked forward to telling John the good news. Upon my return to Kenya in mid-February 1976, John soon confronted me with unsettling news, and a big decision about our future.

Chapter 23:
February 1976 – A New CIA Assignment

I had only been back in Kenya a week when John approached me with the news. 'I have been waiting to tell you this, as I know you have been a little tired from the trip and the time-change. The CIA has a new assignment for us.' I looked at John and saw a look of dejection in his eyes.

'What's the assignment?'

'They want us to move to a new place and take control of a new bugging operation.'

My heart sank. I had grown to love our three-bedroom bungalow. It had a beautiful back garden with green grass, a vegetable garden, a play area for the girls, and several trees and flower beds. The neighborhood was lovely with lots of children that had become friends to our girls.

I tried to stay positive and thought the new house might be suitable for our family. 'Have you seen the new house? Where is it located?'

'I have seen it from the outside, but Jay is going to take us over to view the inside tomorrow. The thing is, it's not a house. It's an apartment and we would inhabit the top floor.'

My heart sank. 'Is the neighborhood nice?'

'Let's talk about it after tomorrow. It's up off Ngong Road on the way to the rugby pitch.'

The next day, we both were quiet as we drove along Ngong Road. I tried to keep an open mind. John turned left off Ngong Road and slowly guided the car down a dirt road. My heart

270

began to sink. A series of two-story apartments were clustered together at the end of the dirt road. Children played barefoot in the dirt road, and we carefully guided our car around them. I saw Jay's Land Rover parked in front of one of the apartments. None of the dwellings had any type of landscaping in front of the units. No grass or flowers. Just dirt.

Jay greeted me with a smile. 'Hi, Linda. Hope you had a nice visit in California, but now it's time to get to work.'

I could have imagined it, but I felt certain I saw a slight smirk on his face. Jay unlocked the outer door of the upstairs' unit and led us up a flight of stairs to the upper apartment. The layout and echo sound of the stairs was similar to our last duplex, but not as nice. I suddenly had visions of Josh falling and cracking his head on the stone steps. The stairs led us to an open sitting room. I let out a quiet gasp when I saw the lounge. Every wall had been painted in a bright color. One wall was black, another was turquoise blue, the third and fourth walls were pink and lime green. I was too stunned to speak.

Jay offered, 'An East Indian family lived here before. You know how they like things colorful. Naturally, we will have the house repainted for you.'

There was stunned silence on my end. Jay gave us a tour of the house, which was half the size of our current home. The kitchen was small, and the apartment possessed only two bedrooms, which meant the three children would have to share.

I was pulled from my stupor when Jay asked. 'What do you think? We have to move quickly on this. The listening device is already in place, and we really need to move you here quickly so we can get started ASAP. Of course, we hope you will make an acquaintance with your new asset.' Jay went on talking, but by this time I was in such a state of shock I heard no more details about the plan.

John asked, 'Would there be quarters for our houseboy, George and his son, Chris?'

'Yes. There is a section down the way for servants, but not attached to the apartment.'

After a few moments John said, 'Well, Jay. Linda and I have a lot to discuss. Could you give us a few days?'

'The agency will need to know soon. We want to have somebody in here by the end of the month. I'll give you the weekend to think about it.'

'Linda and I will discuss it and let you know by Monday.'

Dust flew from the rear of the car as we bounced down the dirt road. We were quiet until we turned right onto Ngong Road. John reached across the seat and took my hand in his. 'What are you thinking, Linda?'

'I'm in a state of shock. Even if we agreed to move over here, how would we explain it to our friends? No one, in their right mind, would downgrade from our present home to live in an upstairs apartment off a dirt road. They would think we had lost our minds. It's not even as nice as the duplex in Hurlingham, and clearly not safe for a toddler. There's no enclosed garden area, no grass, and the girls would miss their friends in our neighborhood. Do you think Jay has an ulterior motive?'

'I'm not sure. It may stem from us not being able to bug Sergei and Mohammed from our present house.'

'John, I swear to you that when I assessed the equipment in the bathroom, the meter said there was enough frequency to continue with the operation. You know I would never lie about that.'

'I know. It could be that they just want us to do more for the agency other than running a safe house, checking post office boxes, and giving parties to meet potential assets. I can't help but wonder if Jay suggested this to stick it to us. It's been pretty clear that we never warmed to him after the rock-climbing incident and him bouncing you all over the back of the rover at seven-months pregnant.'

I chuckled as I recalled the incident. 'I don't know what we can do.'

'Let's sleep on it and weigh our options.'

* * * * * *

We discussed the issue for the better part of the next two days. John was more inclined to take the assignment than me, but in the end we both agreed that our time with the CIA would be coming to an end. We had originally planned to do three tours for NIS, which would have taken us to the summer of 1977. We both agreed that we should let the school know we would not be renewing our contract for the following year and would return to San Diego in the summer of 1976.

The next day, John met with another agent named Paul and sought his counsel. Paul was one of the few agents left from our time with Howard. He had given us a reel-to-reel mixed tape of music. I remember the mixed tape because I was intrigued by one of its songs. The guitarist weaves a story to enlist the help of a telephone *Operator* to get the number of his old girlfriend who dumped him for *his best old ex-friend Ray*. I was amazed at the clever lyrics and tune but did not know the artist's name. Upon returning to California, I discovered the artist was Jim Croce, and was saddened to learn the young singer had died in a plane crash in 1973. It felt like I had lost a friend. To this day, I have been a lifelong Croce fan.

John arrived home just before dinner, and we sat with a glass of wine watching our three children play on the grass. We were both in a pensive mood as we enjoyed the equatorial sun inching toward the west. I thought the plumeria blossoms looked especially lovely in the waning light of the day. My heart had been heavy all throughout the day. We loved our home in Kenya and the many friends we had made at NIS and Harlequins. Neither of us seemed eager to begin the discussion of our future.

'How was your meeting with Paul?'

'Paul assured me that your evaluation of the listening device was never in question. He said that things like that happen from time to time. He had not been to see the new property but cringed when I gave a description of the apartment. I told him that we were grateful for everything Howard and the agency had done for us, but we did not think we could explain to our friends why we would move there. I told him of the dangers of having a toddler with the open stairwell, and the lack of garden space for our girls to play in.'

'Did he understand?'

'I think he did. I told him we would be leaving Kenya in June when the school year ended. I asked if we could stay here for the next four months. I offered to make restitution for the rent. He said he would relay our decision to the agency, and he was certain that restitution would not be necessary. We would continue to be under contract with the CIA until the end of June—operating a safe house and doing the other jobs. He said to leave what furniture was the property of the agency and they would come in and clean and paint the inside of the house for the new tenants.'

"Is the agency going to keep the house?'

'He said he wasn't sure, but it's not likely. They will recycle the furniture to another piece of property.'

'What about Jay?'

'Paul offered to let Jay, and the new Chief of Station know our wishes.'

I asked, 'Are you sad?'

'A little, but I see no other option. Moving to that apartment would have made no sense to anyone. Our friends would think we'd gone mad. We now have four months to enjoy our home and this beautiful country. And, Linda, that's exactly what we're going to do.'

'We'll treasure this time, but it's hard because we're not leaving on our own terms. The decision was made for us, and it's given us little time to process it all.' I looked back at our house and choked back a tear, 'I've loved this house so much.'

'I know you have. We'll be fine.'

We watched the girls climbing on a wooden jungle gym John had built for them for Christmas. Josh was holding a small American football, a gift from our trip home in January. He tossed it up in the air and kicked it across the grass like he was kicking for touch in rugby.

'Oh, I almost forget, we got a letter from your dad today.'

Our mail had always been sent to the post office box used by the school. John pulled it from his jacket pocket and handed it to me.

I opened the envelope. 'Dad has booked his flight and will be here next month. He wants to stay for several months. At least that's something to look forward to.'

The next day, I called my parents and told them we would be leaving Kenya and coming home in early July. They were excited with the news and Dad offered to help us pack up and prepare for our journey home. After his stay in Kenya, Dad said he had booked a flight to Boston where he planned to meet my mom to visit her family. They invited us to meet them there, which would break up the trip for us before heading home to California.

The problem was, we didn't exactly know what that meant for us. We had no job waiting for us and no place to live. The one thing in our favor was a *nest egg* of money that had been put into our bank account for our four years working for the CIA. We had never received a paper trail of the account in Kenya for obvious reasons. We had never touched any of the money during our time with the agency. For the rest of our lives, we would thank Howard and the CIA for helping us resettle in California.

The money in our bank account in San Diego would eventually help us purchase a used car and secure a mortgage on a house when we returned to Southern California. It gave us the time we needed when trying to navigate a teaching job in a saturated market that was inundated with post-Vietnam competition. Eventually, we would have to expand our search to land a teaching position for John in a town called Hemet—a small farming community, which we had never heard of, seventy miles northeast of San Diego in Riverside County.

Chapter 24:
March 1976 – A Last Visit from Bruce

Dad arrived in March. We had communicated our plans to our friends and began preparing for our final departure home. It was wonderful having him with us for three months. We played golf together, while Shauna, who was nearing eight, and Tara. closing in on six, were in school, and Josh under the care of his ayah, Agnus. We were invited to many outings and our friends graciously included Bruce at every farewell dinner and party.

Father Scanlon called on us when he was in Nairobi and talked to Dad about the work the missionary priests were doing in the northern frontier district near Lake Turkana. Father Pat arranged for Bruce to spend a few weeks with the missionary Irish priests and nuns in Turkana, the same region where John had earlier been baptized Catholic. Later, Dad said it was one of the most spiritual experiences of his life, witnessing the selfless work of the priests and nuns working with the Turkana people.

**Dad's photo of an Irish missionary priest saying Mass at
Lake Turkana**

I loved how my father found a unique joy in the people he
met. Dad rarely talked about himself but delighted in asking
questions of others. He taught me so much by example from
the way he lived his life. Dad loved to travel and told me,
'Linda, I came to learn that the best photos are not of the
scenery of the places I visited. The best photos are of the people
I met along my journey.' I loved that he possessed a very
youthful outlook on life and was always eager to try something
new.

During his visit, I celebrated my thirtieth birthday on April
28. Dad I and ventured into the city to spend the day shopping
and going to lunch. As we popped in and out of various shops

in Nairobi, he would peek around an aisle and tease me saying, 'I can't believe I have a daughter who's turning thirty.'

It brought a smile to my face every time he did it. Dad knew that I was entering another decade of my life with a hint of uncertainty about the future. He wanted to lighten the moment and make me laugh.

'Linda, I want to get you something special for your birthday. Something that you will always remember about your thirtieth birthday. Something that will always remind you of our special day together.' I chose a locally made necklace with one large bead in a swirling red, yellow, and black design, which was fastened on a black leather rope. A bracelet with a matching chunky bead on a leather strap completed the set. I have the necklace and bracelet, and to this day, think of him every time I wear it.

In the waning days of our time in Kenya, Dad and our family wanted to see as much of East Africa as possible. Tourists were not going into Uganda because of the unrest with Idi Amin, so we decided to visit the Masai Mara and Tanzania. Over the Easter break, we rented a Volkswagen bus to take one last safari to the Masai Mara and Serengeti Plains. I knew Shauna and Tara would remember some events of their lives in Kenya, but I grieved that my twenty-one-month-old, Josh, would have no memory of the beautiful land we called home for five years.

We packed and were excited to go on one last safari. As it turned out, our poor luck with Volkswagen buses continued to haunt us. We rented a safari bus, with a top that would pop up for open-air viewing of wildlife from Abercrombie and Kent.

On our second night in Tanzania the car broke down because a part broke near the wheel from the jarring motion on the open savanna roads.

No worries—hakuna matata. We rolled the bus off the road and began making camp for the night. Luck prevailed in the afternoon, and John waved down a tour bus heading into the town we had just come from. The African driver said there was a decent garage there that would probably have the part we needed.

I was grateful that Bruce was with us, and we would not have to spend a night alone in the wild. Dad pitched our tent, while the girls and I gathered wood to make a large fire for the night. I was nervous about Josh being so young. I had visions of him being carried off by a hungry lion or a leopard, so Dad suggested Josh and I bunk in the bus.

John hitched a ride into town and came back the following morning with the new part, as we were eating breakfast. He and Dad set about repairing the bus. Fortunately, we had no other problems with the bus for the rest of the trip.

We drank in the beauty of the Masai Mara and Serengeti Plains on that safari. The grass was green from the long rains, and we viewed large herds of zebra and impala grazing in the distance. We saw large prides of lions feasting on the bounty they had killed—lying on their backs in the shade with bloated stomachs. One morning, we stopped in the middle of a flat, grassy area for breakfast. We set up camp chairs outside the bus as I made pancakes and coffee on a camp stove. We had finished our morning meal and lingered with our coffee to enjoy the animals grazing in the distance.

Suddenly, two rangers pulled up in their Land Rover. They were very unhappy.

'Bwana, what are you thinking? You cannot be out of your car in this game park. This is hatari sana—much danger for you.'

We had been safari camping for years in Kenya without an issue. Thinking they were being a little overzealous in their tone, but wanting to comply, John said, 'We are deeply sorry—samahani. We will pack our things and leave now.'

Over our time in Kenya, we had found that most animals, like elephants, giraffes, or zebras, will only allow you to get a certain distance before moving off to a safe distance. Therefore, we were shocked when, at that precise moment and out of the blue, a large Black Rhinoceros came charging through our camp.

The ranger became very animated and began to point and shout at us with an *I-told-you-so* attitude. 'Ah, bwana. Do you see what I am saying? This rhino could have killed you.'

It was as if the incident had been orchestrated for our benefit. The rhino could not have been more than ten yards from the perimeter of our spot. But we knew it was a very real and potential danger. The rangers were extremely proud that their admonition had saved us from the charging rhino. They were absolutely right. Message received. We were packed and were inside the bus within five minutes.

'Daddy, what did we do wrong? That rhino was running fast.'

'I guess we shouldn't have been outside of the bus, Shauna. Rhinos have poor eyesight. They don't like to go near people, but this rhino just didn't see us. The rangers were right in warning us and we now understand our mistake.'

Later that night, as we sat around a roaring campfire on the Serengeti Plains, we could see the reflection of the eyes of elephants and other game in the distance as we reflected on the incident with the rhino. On occasion, we had witnessed a Cape Buffalo, or a young bull elephant charging our car while on a camera safari, but we could not believe that the rhino had chosen that very moment to come so close. It almost seemed as though the rhino had been placed there on cue—like a prop from central casting in a movie. For the rangers, it couldn't have been scripted any better and I'm certain they shared the incident with others for weeks to come.

Dad knew that Josh would not remember much of anything about his time in Kenya and talked about staging a video of Josh by himself with herds of wildlife in the distance.

Shauna said, 'But Grandpa, remember what the rangers said about that.'

'I know, Shauna. And you're absolutely right, but I think if we are careful and position him just for a minute, we could shoot the video, and it would be a great memory for him when he's older.'

We found a beautiful place with animals on the green plains of the Serengeti. Thorn trees and a stream of water flowed in the distance. Dad set up the shot with his video camera, and the girls stayed inside the bus. I stood watch, as John took Josh by the hand and led him away from the bus. He encouraged Josh to stay and look at the camera before stepping out of the shot. It all happened extremely fast, but we were able to enjoy the video of a young boy, seemingly alone, with African animals grazing in the distance.

John with Josh setting up the video for Bruce.

**Camping on the Serengeti Plains in Tanzania
with the pop-up bus**

Chapter 25:
July 1976 – A Last Farewell

After seeing Bruce off at the airport, with the promise to meet him and Esther in Boston in a few weeks, our time was filled with selling household items, cars, and looking for positions for our houseboy, George, his son Chris, and our ayah, Agnus. A couple from Denmark had rented the house and were happy to retain George and Chris with the property. Helping Agnus find employment was harder, but she eventually found a job with a couple from Canada. The three household servants had become like family to us.

I recalled how George had contracted chickenpox from Shauna and Tara the previous year and bore the scars on his face as evidence. What was a childhood disease for the girls became life-threatening for George, who had fewer antibodies to fight that contagious disease. Young Chris, our gardener, had lovingly watched our children at night when we had an engagement. Agnus walked with Josh every afternoon and shared stories of his antics. Josh liked to mimic the African men who loved to stroll along with a walking stick. He always searched the bushes until he found just the right one before he and Agnus set out on their journey.

Agnus loved to give us a daily report on his behavior. 'Memsahib, bwana kidogo—little man—was mbaya sana— very bad today. Another memsahib was walking with her little dog on a leash. The dog barked and was a little kali—angry, as she passed by us. Bwana kidogo tried to hit the little dog with his stick. I told him *hapana*, NO. I made him say sorry for using his walking stick to hit.' Sometimes she would offer praise. 'Joshua was a very good boy today— *mzuri sana.* Bwana kidogo picked these lovely flowers for his mama. I will put them in water for you.'

Josh with walking stick in Ngong Hills—1976

We had meetings with the agency to return the camera and various other items they had loaned us over the course of the years we had worked for them. We were also asked to sign a non-disclosure agreement, using our code names Betsy and Babe one final time. The NDA was a contract stating we would not discuss or write about our employment with the CIA for five years.

Selling off our belongings was like having to shed a favorite coat on a chilly day. The house grew hollow as we advertised and spread our possessions on the back lawn. People came from everywhere to purchase items they needed in a seemingly never-ending cycle of expatriates coming and going in Kenya. Shauna and Tara cried as the other children carted off their toys and jungle gym. Tara had been given a stuffed bear our first year in Kenya. It was tattered and worn, and I had repaired it many times. We had to be judicious in what we packed, and I encouraged her to give it to a neighbor friend, Cecilia. To this day, she reminds me of her feelings about it.

We had a wooden crate built about the size of a square casket to ship the mementos we could not live without. The two small Zanzibar chests we had bought from Fred, the antique brass and copper I had purchased over time on River Road, my lovely banana fiber baskets. Several hand-carved wooden animals and other artifacts were carefully packed inside the crate to be delivered to a shipping yard in Long Beach, California.

We vacated the house in late June and were grateful we had been invited to stay with our dear friends Rob and Sue Evans until our flight out the following week. Our time in Kenya was slowly ebbing away like a hazy dream. I felt like I was coming to the end of a favorite book that made one sad because you never wanted it to end.

When you live abroad, chances are that the friends you made will eventually scatter to various parts of the globe and you will never see them again. This made our eventual parting of the ways extremely sad. From early on, the hub of our social lives had been intertwined with our association with Harlequin Rugby Club. It seemed fitting that our departure coincided with a final game of rugby, which we witnessed as spectators, the afternoon before our scheduled flight home later that evening.

Hugs and more hugs were given to our dearest friends who had come to the airport to see us off. I kept my sadness in check until our plane rose in the air. It was then that I began to sob like reliving the death of a cherished loved one. I was glad it was dark, and I could not see a herd of wildebeest grazing on plains like raisins on a bed of oatmeal. John patted my hand, but we didn't say much. I knew he was grieving in his own way.

Chapter 26:
July 3, 1976 – Trouble at Entebbe Airport

Our five years in Kenya were over. We were filled with sadness leaving our friends and colleagues as we sat on the plane that would take us home to California, knowing we probably would never see this beautiful country again. I knew it was the right time for us to leave Kenya, but still, the ache was like losing a sacred relic that would only exist in the recesses of my memory.

I sighed and looked at the departure board at Embakasi Airport and suddenly froze.

'John, why didn't you tell me our plane stops in Uganda? I thought our flight from Kenya would take us straight to Brussels then to New York?'

'I know, Linda. I found out about it a few days ago. I didn't tell you because…well…I knew you'd worry.'

I looked at my husband and could see the strain on his face. 'Well, I am *very* worried. It's been all over the newspapers. Those poor passengers. They've been held hostage for weeks at Entebbe Airport. There's no telling what that madman, Idi Amin, plans to do with them.' I looked into John's eyes. 'I understand why you didn't tell me but—worried! Quite frankly, with our history with the agency, I'm frantic!'

My heart raced as I held our twenty-one-month-old son, Joshua, in my arms. Our two young daughters, eight-year-old Shauna and six-year-old Tara, played innocently with several children from Kenya Harlequin Rugby Club, who had come with their parents to bid us farewell after five lovely years in Nairobi. The years in Kenya had been wonderful and it was difficult saying goodbye to friends who had become like family to us. We knew that we might never see many of them again.

John gave me a reassuring smile and patted Josh on his head. 'I'm sure our airline wouldn't send us into Uganda if they felt it would put us in danger. It's a quick layover—just to pick up a few more passengers. We should be in and out by 9:00 PM. We probably won't even have to get off the plane. Besides, those hostages are sequestered near the old runway and terminal. They're nowhere near us. We'll be landing on the new runway. It'll be fine.'

How wrong we were. Upon landing in Uganda, military guards armed with rifles, ushered everyone off the plane and into the newly built terminal in Kampala. I was the only person allowed to stay on the plane because our young son was asleep in my arms. I waited, nervously wondering what my husband and two young daughters were doing. After an hour, the crew and passengers were allowed back on board. I looked at my watch, noting that it was a little after 9:00 PM. *Okay we're a little late, but soon we'll be off and away. We still can catch our connecting flight to New York in Brussels.*

Wrong again. When the pilot tried to start the plane, the engine wouldn't turn over. The sluggish noise reminded me of a dying battery. Without warning, all lights and air circulation on the plane were shut off. We sat in darkness, with the air growing stale and dank. No one spoke to us or explained what had gone wrong. After several minutes, we heard the sound of a machine, like a generator, whirling near the outside of the plane. This went on for about forty minutes. As we sat in darkness, there was very little talking. A nervous feeling among the passengers hung in the air like fog.

'What did they do with you inside the terminal?' I whispered to John.

'Well, there are lots of armed soldiers walking around with guns. Several agents looked at our passports. My guy asked why I had entered the country twice without a visa.'

'What did you say?'

'I told him the truth…that I came over with the Harlequins rugby team and forgot that I needed to get one because my British teammates didn't need one. I also told him we were leaving East Africa and going home to the US permanently. He raised an eyebrow but let it pass.'

'Thank God for that,' I whispered. 'The sooner we're out of here the better.'

In time, the whirling sound of the machine finally stopped, and I could hear it being towed away from the plane. The lights came on and immediately one of the flight attendants began walking up and down the aisle liberally showering us with bug spray and announcing that it was a company regulation. Many of the passengers began to cough. I covered my son's face with a light blanket and tried not to cough on him. Thankfully, he continued to sleep peacefully through it all. After a few more minutes, the pilot started the engine, and everyone let out a collective sigh of relief. Several people clapped. As the plane finally began to taxi down the new runway, I looked at my watch and noted that it was 10:00 PM.

Despite an exhausting twenty hours of travel, the rest of the journey went smoothly, and we landed early in New York on the Fourth of July. We were tired from the journey but happy to be finally back on US soil. Going through customs our agent looked at our passports and tickets and whistled.

'You folks sure are lucky.'

John asked, 'What do you mean?'

'I can see by your documents that you were in Uganda last night.'

'Yes, we had a little trouble with the plane but flew out of there by 10:00 PM.'

The agent whistled and said, 'Then you're even luckier than I first thought.'

'What are you saying?' questioned John.

'Last night a group of Israeli soldiers surprised the Ugandan soldiers and terrorists at the old terminal with a sneak attack. They rescued those passengers that had been held hostage sometime before midnight. It's been all over the news!'

John and I looked at each other through wide eyes. The incident had taken place just two hours after our plane left Uganda. Every newspaper reported the events leading up to the attack.

June 27, 1976, Entebbe: Four Palestinian terrorists hijack an Air France Airbus in

Athens, Greece. With approval from Ugandan dictator, Idi Amin, the terrorists divert the plane to Entebbe Airport in Uganda. Eight terrorists separate all Jewish and Israeli hostages. The remaining non-Jewish passengers are released. The flight crew bravely opts to stay behind with the remaining passengers. A series of petitions are made, including a demand that forty Palestinian militants, held in Israel, be exchanged for the hostages. Israel opens negotiations in an effort to stall, but secretly refuses to give in to the terrorists' demands. 'Operation Thunderbolt' is conceived and executed on July 3 at 11:59 PM.

After a quick refueling stop in Kenya, four planes land on the old Entebbe runway just before midnight. To confuse the soldiers, a black Mercedes, identical to President Idi Amin's car, and two jeeps emerge from the first plane. Within six minutes, three other planes land on the old runway. Airport personnel and soldiers appear confused. Israeli soldiers enter the terminal and gunfire ensues. One Israeli soldier, Yonatan Netanyahu,* is killed almost immediately. Five other soldiers become wounded. Three Jewish hostages are slain in the crossfire. All eight terrorists are killed within six minutes.

In twenty minutes, the hostages and crew are evacuated onto one of the planes and depart from the old runway. The remaining rescue teams quickly board the other planes and depart. The entire operation takes 58 minutes. On hearing the news, the madman Idi Amin becomes enraged and murders an older woman who is sick and has been sequestered at a local hospital. *Yonatan was the older brother of Benjamin Netanyahu, the current Prime Minister of Israel.

I looked at John and shook my head. 'We're lucky to be alive. Maybe luckier than people will ever know.'

'I'm sorry, Linda. I would never have placed my family in harm's way if I had known.'

'It's not your fault. I wonder if the agency was in on the plan. I would suspect that they were, but we'll never know for sure.'

We were exhausted as we retrieved our luggage at the baggage area at Kennedy Airport. It was midafternoon and we had to wait hours to board our connecting flight to Boston. After discovering our narrow escape from the customs agent about the raid on Entebbe, we thanked the Lord that we hadn't gotten stranded in Uganda. We found a pay phone at the airport and called my parents, who were staying with relatives in Cape Cod. They did not know about our detour in Uganda, and we decided to wait to share the news. We told them our plane would arrive at 8:00 PM. They assured us they would make the two-hour drive from the cape to meet us at Logan Airport. That never happened.

Our flight from Kenya seemed to be fraught with trouble from the start. The turmoil seemed to mirror our unsettled feelings leaving the land we had loved so much. Traveling with three children is hard but overall, they did well. After a layover in Brussels, we boarded our connecting flight to New York on July 4, 1976. America was celebrating its two-hundred-year bicentennial becoming a republic. The airport crackled with excitement. Passengers dressed in red, white, and blue and holding American flags, which fluttered like colorful butterflies, rushed to their various gates.

We decided to get a bite to eat at one of the airport restaurants. John and I spoke in hushed tones about what might have happened to us if the plane had not been able to start. Playing rugby for Harlequins, John had entered Uganda without a visa…twice! The British players didn't need a visa, and no one thought that John might need one as an American citizen. Both times he was allowed entry but was told it was a 'Prohibitive Entry' which meant he was allowed in the country but without the proper credentials. We wondered if the plane had been detained and they had delved into our lives further, they might have discovered that we had not only been employed at Nairobi International School, but we also had worked undercover for the CIA for the past four years.

For us, the afternoon seemed to drag on, and we were delighted to board American Airlines for the last leg of our journey to Boston. The flight should have been an easy one, but it wasn't. We groaned when the pilot said there was trouble at Logan Airport, and we would have to circle Boston airport until we were given permission to land. The plane flew in circles for two hours. Day turned to night, and we could see masses of fireworks blanketing the land from the windows of the plane, as our country hailed the two-hundredth anniversary of our Independence Day. Our flight attendants knew we had come from Kenya and had been traveling for two days. They were so kind to us.

At 9:00 PM the captain spoke to us over the speaker. 'I'm sorry to report that there has been a bomb scare at Logan Airport. We are diverting the plane to Connecticut. You will be put in a hotel and another flight will take you into Logan tomorrow morning.'

John and I looked at each other through weary eyes. I was too tired to cry.

Epilogue:
Our New Life in Hemet, California

The first few months after returning home were difficult. The Vietnam war had recently ended, and teaching jobs were hard to come by. To avoid the draft, countless college students had decided to go into teaching. Over the summer of 1976 in San Diego, John interviewed for positions that sometimes held a pool of one hundred applicants.

We decided to expand our search to Riverside County and John found a job teaching in the sleepy little farming community of Hemet, California. Hemet is seventy miles north of San Diego. Thanks to our service with the CIA, we were able to buy a used Toyota station wagon and put a down payment on a modest three-bedroom house in a working-class neighborhood.

We decided Shauna, who was eight, would occupy one bedroom and six-year-old Tara and two-year-old Josh would occupy the other bedroom. The girls were enrolled in Ramona Elementary, which was within walking distance for them. Life was settling into place.

We were back to a single car, which John needed for work. I needed a form of transportation, so we purchased a white bicycle at Sears for fifty-nine dollars. John attached a basket to the handlebars, and a toddler seat on the back for Josh. The bike was Josh and my main source of transport around town for the next two years. Together, we would ride to the supermarket to buy food. I could fit a paper bag in the basket and Josh carried the second bag on his lap wedged against my back. If we wanted to visit the park, we biked there and back. On one teacher's salary, money was limited, but Josh and I rode the bike all over the city, amusing ourselves with things we could manage at little cost. Hemet was a small, flat valley town, so the biking system worked well. I know I was in decent shape during those years.

When Josh turned four, John and I made the decision that I should complete my graduate studies to begin teaching full time. The investment would increase our income, which was tight. We put a down payment on a used Honda Civic, and Josh and I made the one-hundred-mile round trip to the University of San Bernardino to finish my degree, while Josh attended on-campus day care. Thankfully, Josh was a good traveler.

Soon, I was hired at Ramona Elementary to teach fourth grade. Our lives began to settle in place, and we came to love the town and the friends we were gradually making there. Like Kenya, our lives centered around John coaching football and baseball. The wives of these coaching men became central to our social entertainment.

John heard of a rugby team in San Bernardino and drove forty miles to inquire about joining. After the first practice, the team quickly realized that John knew much more about the fundamentals of the sport than anyone. When he arrived home, he told me he had not only made the team, but they had also made him team captain.

I knew Josh would never have any memories of his life in Kenya. I wanted him to be proud of his place of birth and have a connection to it. At night, when I tucked him in bed, I would tell him a serialized story of a little boy named Josh, who was separated from his parents in Kenya. The lost boy was befriended by multiple animals who guarded over him. Yes, it may have been inspired by the *Jungle Book*, but we made it our own. There was Zebby the Zebra, Leo the Lion, and a cast of other characters that shared Josh's adventures in the forests of Kenya.

I have always been a storyteller. It was a gift inherited from my dad, Bruce, who was an amazing storyteller. As children, Dad would tell us bedtime stories about a group of characters that lived in the sea. There was Benny the Seal and Willy the Whale. We looked forward to the fascinating adventures of these stories. I believe I became a good storyteller through him.

I was talking to my long-time friend, Sue Evans, in England recently. We reminisced about our extraordinary time in Kenya, noting the country had only been formed as a republic for seven years when the Allisons first arrived there in 1971. We agreed that it was an unusual time period for Kenya, which was caught between two distinct cultures. The country was transitioning from the twilight of Colonial Kenya, to embracing the dawn as the new and independent Republic of Kenya.

During our time, the population of Nairobi was a mere 645,000 people. It was not unusual to see Kenya's new president, Jomo Kenyatta, parade through the city in a convertible car waving his fly-whisk—a mark of authority in Kenyan culture. The entire country of Kenya was small, with thirteen million in population. Today, Kenya continues to expand at fifty-five million people, with four and a half million people inhabiting the capital of Nairobi.

Sue and I recalled the iconic cylindrical Hilton Hotel, where we shared many evenings of dining and dancing with John and Rob. The Hilton was Nairobi's first skyscraper—which was opened by Jomo Kenyatta in 1969. Sadly, it closed its doors in 2022. The nights of dining and dancing with friends at the Hilton are just memories of the past. People tell us not to go back. We wouldn't know it. It's not the sleepy city we once knew. Better to keep the memories frozen in that unique time period of the seventies.

Skyline of Nairobi from Ngong Road—1972

I once heard it said: Africa changes you forever, like nowhere on earth. Once you have been there, you will never be the same. That was true for me. It was a gift to experience it.

* * * * * *

While driving in Nairobi, Josh loved to sit on my lap and gaze out the car window, with vibrant anticipation in his eyes. We could drive five miles out of the city and regularly see giraffes, zebras, and gazelles grazing on vegetation by the side of the road. The sight never ceased to amaze us, and we shared in our little boy's joy.

When we arrived back in the states, we often made the seventy-mile journey from Hemet to San Diego to visit Grandma Sue, Bruce, Esther, and our families. Two-year-old-Josh would perch himself on my lap—in the days before seatbelts and car seat laws—and look intently out the window. I knew what he was looking for and it broke my heart. This went on for about a month until finally he just gave up. I understood he had finally come to realize, other than an occasional cow, there were no exotic animals on the sides of the freeways in California. We understood and shared his sadness. *I feel your pain, bwana kidogo. We miss it too.*

**Linda and Josh on Ngong Hills overlooking
the Great Rift Valley—1976**

Author's Notes

- John Allison died December 7, 2007 from a massive heart attack while golfing with his Crawford High School friends in Scottsdale, Arizona. The night before he died, we talked of the roads he would take after the tournament to visit his friend and former Harlequin rugby player, Simon Walton, in Las Vegas. Sadly, Simon learned of John's passing upon his return to England. John taught and coached for thirty-seven years. He retired from teaching in June 2007 and passed away six months later at the age of sixty-three. I received countless letters and emails from former students and friends in Kenya and the United States. Hundreds of friends, family, and former students attended his memorial service. It was a life well-lived, but all too short.

- Shauna Allison Neuenswander lives with her husband Dwayne in Payson, Arizona. Shauna retired from California Family Life Center, as an administrator, where she supervised troubled girls aged twelve to eighteen in Hemet. Shauna and Dwayne are active in their church, where Shauna works part time. They are energetic retirees, and love hiking in the surrounding mountains with their dog, Jeckel.

- Tara Allison McTaggart lives in Aguanga, California with her son, Curran. Curran's hobbies include working out at the gym to stay fit. Her husband, Ken, died in a skydiving accident as an instructor in 2010. Tara is an accomplished professional artist. She runs *Terra Bella Lavender Farm* and a private hair salon on her five-acre property with her dog, Indigo, and cats Holly and Willow.

- Joshua Allison and wife Lisa live in Florence, Arizona, with son Noah and dog Porter. Lisa teaches kindergarten and Josh creates and sells unique sterling silver jewelry and handcrafted woodwork and flips houses for resale. Josh brews crafted beer as a hobby. Noah graduated from high school as an accomplished baseball player. He has accepted a full Division 1 baseball scholarship to Cochise College near Douglas, Arizona.

- Linda Shields Allison Mars retired from teaching in 2008. She married her high school sweetheart and surfer boyfriend, Russell Mars, in 2015. Russell's wife, Janet, passed away from cancer seven months after John in July 2008. After forty-three years, Russell and Linda reunited through a longtime friend, Terry Nettles Meaney, as a grief support system for each other. In an unusual coincidence, Terry also introduced Linda to John at a birthday party in 1967. Russell and Linda call her *the messenger*.

- A special thanks to those who contributed to this memoir: Christopher Bane, Sue Evans, John and Jan Ellis, Tom Simpson, Robert Mazelow, Frank Matsalia, Mark Wiley, Laura and Barbara Schlesinger and many more.

- A very special thanks to Howard, Anita and Chris Bane. We are forever grateful for the gift of your friendship. You certainly made our lives in Kenya interesting and through your grace, gave us a boost to begin our life anew in the United States.

- Many of our Harlequin friends have passed away, but they live in the memories of a unique time and place in our lives called Kenya: Robert Evans, Norman Wiley, John Maynard, Father Patrick Scanlon, Roy and Lynette Warren, Dougie and Margaret Hamilton, Howard and Anita Bane, Bill Stanley, and so many more.

- A special thank you to my contact at the Central Intelligence Agency for his invaluable help in advising me on what I could and could not say in this memoir. Please note that some of the names in this memoir have been changed for security reasons.

www.ingramcontent.com/pod-product-compliance
Lightning Source LLC
LaVergne TN
LVHW051923260125
802203LV00001B/171